TRY NOT TO LAUGH

D K POWELL

Shopno Sriti Media

Try Not To Laugh

(How to Revise, Memorise and Survive Exams)

A Guide for students

D K Powell

Published by Shopno Sriti Media

ISBN 978-0-9957121-3-3

Contents

Dedication	7
Introduction	9
Part I – Getting ready	
Chapter 1 – Why you need this book	19
Chapter 2 – How our brains work	27
Chapter 3 – Preparing the ground	47
Part II – The Memory Story System	
Chapter 4 – Memory Stories (or how to Memorise stuff)	63
Chapter 5 – Memorising numbers	86
Chapter 6 – Memorising languages	96
Chapter 7 – Memorising people	104
Chapter 8 – Taking it further	112
Appendix – Magic Tricks	123
Acknowledgements	135
About the Author	137
About the Illustrator	139

Dedication

This book is dedicated to all my students at LAMB English Medium School, Bangladesh who I taught from August 2006 until October 2013. You guys, above all others through my teaching career, were the test subjects for the methods contained in this guide. For this - and for many, many hours of crying with laughter together - I thank you from the bottom of my heart. It was an honour to serve you. And I apologise profusely for the long, long wait. Memorising I can do; time management, I can't.

DKP

The three stages of Writer

Introduction: IMPORTANT - READ THIS FIRST

Two middle-aged couples are old friends and get together every month or two to play card games - usually Bridge. On one particular occasion, everything begins as normal. One couple arrives at the others' home, bottle of wine in hand, drinks and nibbles sorted, everyone settles down at the card table, playing partners assigned and an hour or so of earnest Bridge-playing takes place.

They take a break, as usual, and the ladies trot off to the kitchen to sort refreshments leaving the gentlemen to natter at the table.

"Well George," says Tom to his old friend, "I have to say I was very impressed with your playing tonight!"

"Oh yes, old sport?" replies George. "Why so, Tom?"

"Well, not to put too fine a point on it, you're normally not that hot at remembering anything. You know it's true, old bean."

"Oh, not doubting it for a minute, Tom! You know what my memory is like..."

"Precisely, George! But tonight, you've been on fire. Honestly, you've followed the cards perfectly, recalled what suits were called for trumps each time, followed the leads, didn't get confused - you were like a new man!"

George smiled at his friend and then leaned over the table conspiratorially.

"I'll let you into a secret," he said quietly, "I've been using a new memory technique. It's absolutely brilliant! I can remember so much more than I used to."

"My goodness - how remarkable! Well, it has certainly worked for you from what I've seen tonight," Tom admitted. "What's the name of this remarkable memory technique?"

George sat back and furrowed his brow with concentration.

"Oh now…I can do this…hold on."

He thought a moment longer and then said, "Right, I am thinking of a flower…it has leaves, petals…thorns…it's a red flower…"

"Rose?" his friend suggested.

"Rose! That's it!"

George turned round and shouted in the direction of the kitchen.

"Rose," he said, "what's the name of that memory technique I'm using?"

Welcome to the world of memorising. You're about to start an exciting adventure into the depths of your mind. This book holds the power to potentially change your life for the better. I know this because these techniques have changed my life - I am the 'George' mentioned in the joke above. My memory is so bad I've actually forgotten many of the terrible moments where I've forgotten stuff! I've forgotten my name, my kids' birthdays, what I was doing just seconds ago...don't ask me to order food at a restaurant for everybody. I will have forgotten every single order by the time I reach the bar - I've done it many times. Memory techniques then, have been lifesavers for me, over the last thirty years.

So, I know that the techniques you're about to learn work in real life - my own - and I've also helped countless students to improve their memories too. From little children through to middle-aged adults, almost everyone can benefit from at least one or two techniques in this book; let alone the whole system.

But there's a catch - and you need to be very aware of it from the start.

In fact, if you're reading this before buying the book, read all of this introduction now before you part with your cash (you are buying this book, aren't you?). This applies even if you're looking at several books on memory techniques. Sorry, if you bought it already - nothing I can do about that! Anyway, I'm about to tell you something pretty much few, if any, of the others will.

It's this:

There's no quick fix to memorising. All memorising is hard work and needs time, persistence and effort.

There. I've said it. Now let me unpack it before you put this book down and give up any hope of finding an effective system to help you with that exam, or learn that language, or just remember your blasted phone number - and the birthdays of your parents which you always forget. There is hope. You can improve your memory and this book really can help. Just don't think it'll be wham, bam, thank you ma'am. It's more complex than that.

There's no doubt about it: the stuff in this book works. I've used it all myself for more than thirty years. I've taught it to students for over twenty. If you apply the techniques explained here, you will massively increase the speed and efficiency of your recall of information in exams and elsewhere. Furthermore, you'll have a comprehensive system to use to guide your revision and study time which you can apply even years before your exams (in fact, you *should*).

And it will be fun too. That's why this book is called *'Try Not to Laugh'*.

I have told my students for the last two decades that this should be their only problem when they take those pesky exams: laughing. It's not really the done thing in an exam hall, is it? But imagine if that really was your *only* problem? Recalling information should never be an issue for my pupils who have faithfully followed the system these pages will teach you; only preventing sniggering during a test and trying not to get thrown out for disrupting the examination should be the concern! Honestly, I've had lessons where the class and I have been memorising utterly boring Chemistry equations together and we've been literally crying with laughter as we've done it.

But while memory techniques are a way of hot-wiring the brain to learn things fast, they are not an easy quick-fix. You don't get instant recall with no effort. That's what those other books want you to believe and they're wrong. In fact, I'll go so far as to say most of them are deceiving you. It's the reason most people end up giving up on memory techniques: the promise of easy memorising proves false.

Building a house

Have you ever noticed a house, or some other building, being constructed? When I lived in Bangladesh for a few years, I saw construction sites which made my eyes pop! Dhaka, the capital city is, in many ways, one big construction site - there are thousands of buildings being built everywhere. But what you won't see, as a rule, is any kind of scaffolding; at least not as we think of it here in western countries, with metal bars held together with strong nut-and-bolt locking mechanisms and wooden planks used for standing on at various layers. In Bangladesh, you're more likely to see huge concrete floors held up by - I kid you not - bamboo poles. You'll see labourers precariously balanced 20 floors up on ladders made of bamboo too, with no safety harnesses. Sometimes they fall off.

One workman did just that while my family and I were having a meal in a restaurant opposite. It was like something out of a cartoon. We were sipping our drinks and *WALLOP*! A body drops out of the sky and into the skip at the bottom. Equally like a cartoon, the guy got up and wobbled off, dazed but incredibly otherwise unhurt despite falling from at least ten storeys. The stuff in the skip must have cushioned the blow. It was bizarre. We just stared at each other with looks on our faces as if to say: 'Did you just see that too?'

Although most of these buildings stay up okay, it's a nightmare for health and safety. And sometimes, they don't stay up at all. There have been too many instances of buildings collapsing or burning to the ground because of shoddy construction. Over in my home country, the UK, we might take longer to build things (just how many tea breaks does a builder need, I wonder?), but we at least put proper scaffolding up. The metal poles are often the first thing you see being built and then, slowly but surely, you see the construction start to take place. Eventually, the roof is on, the windows are fitted, the walls are painted and…voila!...we have a fish. I'm sorry, I meant a house. I got distracted. In fact, why was I telling you all about what little I know about the construction industry? Oh yes - scaffolding.

You see, our memory is rather like the building made without scaffolding: it's quick but can easily come apart under pressure. Our memory needs scaffolding to work effectively. A more traditional term for this might be called a 'system of recall' - a method for retrieving the memories you have. You'll know this every time you look at an old photo and the memories of what you did that day come flooding back. Or when a friend says, 'Do you remember when...?' and suddenly things you'd completely forgotten come right back into your mind. In order to be certain of remembering things consistently, you need scaffolding in place to help you get the foundations fixed. One day, you might be able to take the scaffolding away. When you do, you'll have a house that will stand for a long time. That's what this system is all about.

But that *doesn't mean it is easy*. For reasons which I'll explain in the next chapter, the only way you will memorise any data is by making your brain work for it. There are many books on the market offering memory techniques (the proper name is *mnemonics*) and almost all of them make it sound like they unlock your mind's potential to make it easy for you to remember anything you wish too. Unfortunately, too often these books are left unused and students go back to desperately hoping they can cram the information into their heads somehow. That's because most mnemonic specialists try to peddle a particular method or idea and don't tend to look at the whole picture. This book is very different for exactly that reason. You'll get both an overall, cohesive system *and* the details you need. You'll learn too how to adapt it all for your own needs.

What I'm offering you here is:

- *A fully comprehensive system to help you memorise almost anything you wish and to adapt and evolve it to meet your own circumstances and needs.*
- *A system which is easy to apply, efficient and fun.*
- *A system which saves you time and effort and gives you focus.*
- *A system which will give you complete confidence in the exam room, knowing you can recall any information you need without fear of forgetting some or all of it.*
- *A system which allows you to structure your revision and memorising from the first day of study until the exam itself.*

But - brilliant though all this is - it doesn't mean you don't have to work. No point having scaffolding if you're then going to swing from a bamboo ladder or never get around to start building walls out of bricks and mortar! More fool you if you fall and crash to the ground and give up any hope of succeeding. You will have to keep using these techniques every day to make them stick. If you persevere, then my system will help you memorise a lot more than you could otherwise - and do so with confidence. And - don't forget - it will be fun (or at least a lot more fun than just reading your books or copying out facts over and over again would be). The hard work of memorising no one can take away. But the right method will be consistent, easy to use and efficient. And - did I say already? - it can also be fun!

So, if you're ready to take the business of revision and study seriously, come join me and learn how to do it really, really well. Prepare to be amazed at just what your mind can do...

"Rose, what's the name of that memory technique?"

Part I – Getting ready

Chapter 1 – Why you need this book

If you are anything like me, then you find studying a real chore. I used to hate revising, but I hated failing exams even more! So, over many years, I started finding out how to make revising easier. Some things I read in books, some things I figured out for myself, but *ALL* the techniques you will learn in this book I use for myself in my day-to-day work as teacher, educational consultant and writer. You're looking at the culmination of around thirty years of research and practice both as a lifelong learner (as I write, I've just completed courses on bookkeeping, neurology and hieroglyphics. Don't ask why. Just. Don't. Ask.) and as a teacher who has trained thousands of students.

Did you ever see the film *'The Matrix'*? If so, do you remember when the main character, Neo, is plugged into the system and has whatever he needs to learn instantly 'downloaded' into his mind? Oh boy, how I wish we could do that! Of course, if we could, I wouldn't need to write this book – but what a great dream that would be to just know anything you wanted. I won't lie to you: this course will not make remembering so easy that it feels like you are in the Matrix. You will need to put effort into learning and using these techniques. They will seem odd at first and you will need some time to even believe they can work at all. But, once you have trained up your 'mind muscles', this course is going to leave you as close to that Matrix feeling as it is possible to be – until they invent it for real, of course.

The Lesson from hell

I came into the classroom and saw my usual happy smiling faces beaming up at me. Teaching my Grade 9 class was such a pleasure. And I'm not even being ironic.

"Good morning guys," I said cheerfully. "Today, in our Chemistry lesson we're going to look at tests for salts and gases."

Every single face changed - at the same instant - from happy beaming grins to looks of horror and disgust. We'd tackled this subject before, and everyone knew it was horrid. Testing for different substances is a nightmare. A seemingly endless list of random things mixed together to turn equally random colours or forms. At Grade 9 level, it makes no sense and feels impossible to keep the complex information in the memory. I knew at that point that this was not going to be our usual fun lesson. This was going to be the lesson from hell. I would be teaching stuff that no one wanted to learn and that I didn't want to teach. To be honest, working out what stuff goes with what colour and with what liquid just does not get me excited.

It is, in a word, *boring*.

But...it had to be learnt. It was in the syllabus for the exam and I knew that there was a huge question each year that looked at 'tests for salts'; it was too big to decide to ignore. What's more, there were lots of little questions spread through all three exams for Chemistry that would ask questions related to this subject. The students had to learn it and I had to teach it.

So, I took a deep breath and said to the students, "Sorry guys, I know you don't want to do this and if there was any other way I could do this I would. But there isn't, and we're just gonna have to slog through the chapter." But then I had a brilliant idea.

And what I did next changed how I thought about science and how I taught my lessons.

By the time the lesson ended, not only did my students understand more about 'tests for salts and gases' better than any of my students had before, but we had spent most of the lesson in tears of laughter! It turned out not to be the lesson from hell, but one of the best lessons I had ever taught. Wow!

That was many years ago now. These days I don't tend to have horrible lessons like I thought that would be (and never for long if I do). Instead, I now say to my students, at the beginning of the course "the most difficult thing you will have to learn to do over the next two years, is learn how not to laugh out loud when you are in the exam!" Honestly, when my students take exams these days, it is the only thing I worry about and pray, '*Please* don't let them be disqualified for disrupting the exam with raucous laughter.'

What this book will teach you...

Do you struggle to remember dates and numbers and specific data?

Do you find yourself too bored to carry on reading that textbook chapter you're supposed to revise for an exam the next day?

Do you get annoyed with yourself that even after spending hours trying to remember something, a few days later it's just gone from your head and you know you've wasted your time?

If so, this book is for you.

Over the next few chapters I will show you:

- *How to improve your memory just by what you eat and drink.*
- *How to remember everything you ever need in any academic subject without having to write anything down – ever – if you don't want to.*
- *How your mind works so you know the secrets for putting information in there and keeping it there.*
- *How to build up a study habit so you never need to panic revise for an exam again.*
- *How to save time so you can see your friends – in fact, how they can help you to remember stuff and how you can help them back.*
- *How to make studying fun and never have boring hours of revising again – in fact I ~~forbid you~~ highly recommend you spend no more than 20 minutes at a time revising!*
- *How to get so used to using these techniques that in the end...you can ignore them! That's right – if you learn the secrets*

in this book well, you won't need them anymore! Well, at least not until the next exam...

...what it won't do...

I have to say, right at the beginning that I am assuming you already know the stuff you want to learn.

What's the point in a book that tells you about things you already know? Well, because there's a difference between understanding principles, methods, dates etc., and keeping all that in your memory. This book is a guide on how to get it to stay in your head – not on how to understand it in the first place. I will give a little advice about that, but this book assumes that you've studied your course(s), understood the text, the lesson, the principles or whatever and that the words all make sense to you. From there, we can get on with making sure it stays in your head.

So, if you have not yet started your course or chosen studies yet – put this book away until you've begun learning stuff. If you are trying to teach yourself (and good for you if you are) then you will need other books to make sure you understand the subject material because this book assumes you already 'get it'.

Pity your teachers

I've been teaching students in the UK for more than 25 years. I've worked as a private tutor, giving lessons one-to-one and I've taught classes of more than 30, at times where nearly half of them had special needs or behavioural problems. For five years, I worked 5,000 miles away from the UK in Bangladesh teaching Science and Maths (among several other subjects) to kids aged 4 to 18. For more than fourteen years, I've been advising teachers all over Asia on how to help their students really learn well. I've been inspected by colleagues, head teachers, other students, government officials and parents more times than I can count. I've helped improve departments and even whole schools, and I've inspected and assessed hundreds of teachers across many subjects.

I can tell you, whether you like your teachers or not, they are probably doing a good job. But good is not always enough. I have had times where I wished I could just teach my older students for every lesson in the timetable, every week, to make sure they get ready for an exam I know they can pass – but then they would fail their other subjects, wouldn't they?! There is just not enough time to do everything and most teachers are beating a countdown to teach you what you need to learn in time for the date the exam is set.

What's more, most teachers were taught by teachers themselves who were also trying to squeeze in as much knowledge as they could in an impossibly short space of time. Not many have been taught anything more than a few basic ideas about how to study, revise and remember the facts they were learning. The fact that they went on to get a degree and train to become teachers means that, somehow, they managed to do it - but some will have scraped by and others walked it with ease. Some will have spent hours revising and killing themselves to remember it all. Others, annoyingly, will have found it terribly easy and never felt an exam was any trouble at all.

I'm sorry to say but both kinds of teachers are bad news for you. Those that slogged away for hours in their youth will think that you need to spend hours and hours equally slogging through textbooks and writing out notes again and again. It will be seen as a horrid but necessary rite of passage. And the justification is always the same: *Everyone has had to do it this way.*

Let me tell you now - ***you don't have to work hard like this***.

The second kind of teacher sees no reason why you can't learn all this stuff – after all, they did it easily themselves. They expect unreasonable amounts of facts to be learnt in a very short space of time and might even get cross with you when you struggle. They certainly don't give you any advice about how to remember it all. They just expect you to do it. They probably don't say that to you. They probably just give you that withering look which makes you feel as though you must be really dumb or something. If you can't remember it, you're surely not trying. *You must be lazy*.

Let me tell you, assuming you've read this far and understood everything, you're not dumb, nor are you lazy. *You can memorise stuff.*

You don't need to worry about either kind of teacher any longer. This course has been designed to 'fill the gaps' and teach you what your own teachers don't have time or the experience to teach. I've made this course compulsory as a subject in its own right at schools where I've had some control of the curriculum, but it is very unusual to find a school willing to do that when so many subjects are battling for space in the school schedule. Even so, I have to fight every year, to keep it in, despite the evidence of how well it works. Teachers just assume that the kids can remember this stuff – after all, they have been getting students to pass exams for years, right? But few teachers take the time to listen to students and realise just how hard it is for them to remember this stuff.

This course has just made the job a whole lot easier for you...

What you need for this course

So, I've told you what you can expect from this course and why you need it. Now it's time I told you what I expect from you.

- *Be prepared to work at the exercises and the examples I'm going to give you.*
- *Have a notebook to hand - or better still the accompanying textbook which is the companion to this book ready by your side. You will need it to follow the techniques I'm going to give you.*
- *Be ready to set aside a little time each day to practise the techniques. They are not hard, and they should be fun if you do them correctly, but they will be unusual and, like exercising*

muscles you've not used before, your brain will 'ache' a little bit as you get used to thinking in a very different way.

- *Don't expect a 'quick fix'. You may be stunned just how easy it is to remember things when you read this course – but don't be fooled. As the section on 'Memorising the Memory Aids' will teach you, it is easy to think you have something permanently memorised when actually you don't.*
- *Most important – I expect you to bring your imagination with you. In fact, the success or failure of this course for you personally will depend entirely on how much you are prepared to take risks and allow your imagination to go wild. You need to be prepared to be a big kid to get the best out of this book. Get ready to think of wild, crazy things - even rude things! But definitely, funny things...the funnier the better. In chapter four you'll see why.*

Well, that's it. We're ready to begin our adventure into hijacking the memory. I hope you find it fun and interesting. I know you'll find it useful. Whilst this is no matrix-style of learning and some effort is going to be needed, I promise you that learning facts will never be the same again if you will faithfully carry out the simple instructions in these pages. Good luck!

That exam you are about to take? It's about to become so much easier…

EXERCISE:

If you're studying subjects now you know you're struggling to remember, start making a list of the various areas you'd like to memorise and know more securely. Try to make them small and specific rather than broad. So, not 'All of Biology' or 'Tudor history'. Write 'the names of veins and arteries running to and from the heart' or 'key dates of the reign of Elizabeth I'. It doesn't have to be a comprehensive list - indeed don't try. Write the top areas which are weighing on your mind. These are the ones you will start tackling first as you learn the memory system.

Chapter 2 – How our brains work

"Neurons that fire together, wire together" (Dr. Jon Medina, *Brain Rules*, 2009)

How does that spongy mess of cells in our head convert thoughts, sight, smells, sounds, taste and touch into memories? Just what is a memory anyway?

I'm not going to bore you with long-winded details of the physiology of the brain for several reasons:

- You can look it up yourself (the power of Google!);
- Much of what we 'know' about the brain is actually little more than educated guesswork. It's really difficult to see what's going on in an alive brain and the physiology is staggeringly complex. Most of our 'knowledge' is actually theory based on extensive research that sometimes baffles as much as it illuminates;
- Lastly, you don't really need to know too much. But a few details will help you better understand why this system works.

So, I'm going to tell you just a little bit of the theories of memory and how the mind works. It'll be reasonably accurate but...new research is coming all the time and old research inevitably goes out of date. So, I'm going to keep it basic.

Once Upon a Time...

Let me tell you a story. Get used to this – I'm going to tell you a lot of stories! I want you to visualise this tale in your mind. Concentrate! - I will want you to remember as much of it as you can afterwards. Are you sitting comfortably? Then we'll begin...

Imagine you're in someone's front room. You can see their baby son playing with silver-coloured balls on the floor. Suddenly an exquisitely beautiful lady walks into the room and picks up some of the balls. You follow her as she goes through the house and out into the back garden where she hurls the balls onto the ground. The balls are bombs! They explode on hitting the ground and send clumps of soil and dirt flying everywhere. Some of the earth goes over the fence and into the neighbour's house and makes a mess of his garden. He's furious! He's a small, round, red-faced man who's really shouting at the woman for the mess she's made. But his fire is soon put out because, who should appear out of the sky but...superman? Well, sort of. This superhero looks more like a huge god out of Roman mythology but he's wearing superhero clothes with the letters SUN written across his chest. Weirdly, there' a little cartoon dog sitting on his shoulder. At this point, you decide to back off from this strange group and leave before anything more bizarre occurs...

How did you get on? Can you remember all the major details? Can you retell the story accurately without looking? I've often told this story and find, on average, that almost every person can get 80-90% of correct after just one telling. Over 50% can tell the story flawlessly. This, despite the fact that the tale makes no sense and feels more like a trippy dream someone had after eating too much cheese the night before. If you haven't remembered all the details, go over the story again a couple of times. It doesn't take long; just make sure you pay attention to the bits you missed.

No, really. Go read it again and make sure you're imagining all the parts. I'm going to wait...

Got it sorted? Good - let's continue.

The odd thing is, you'll probably be able to recall all or most of this story, without ever having to practice or reread it, next week. There's a good chance you'll be able to piece it together even if I asked you to tell the tale a month later. You might need some prompts to get you started and you might have to write it down, filling in bits you missed as they come back to you while you progress through the tale. This is perfectly normal. So why can we remember a nonsense story so well? Is it just this particular story?

In fact, the story isn't nonsense at all (well...okay, yes it is, but there's a purpose to it). You've just memorised something and it might surprise you what it is (well done, if you've already guessed it).

Before I explain what the story means however, I want to explain why it works so well. To do that, I need to tell you a little about how our brains work. Don't skip this bit - understanding how memory works physically is very important for you to grasp how the memory system I will teach you works. There's hard work ahead and I want you to understand why that work is necessary. It's helpful to know just how your brain works, why we forget things and how we remember them too. You will be more motivated to follow the system when you understand these things.

The Brilliant Brain

Most organisms, over a certain size, have what can be easily recognised as a brain. It is a phenomenal piece of engineering by evolution which has taken millions of years to develop. The human brain is, arguably, the very peak of this engineering. Our brain has only been recognisably ours for the last 200,000 years, roughly. One of the key details of what sets ours apart from the rest of the animal kingdom is its size. Somewhere along the way, our DNA mutated consistently over many generations to give more and more importance to this squidgy stuff shoved into our craniums. This kicked off around 800,000 years ago.

Oddly, the human brain has actually shrunk during that last 200,000 years - not hugely, but significantly. Why? No one is entirely sure (nothing much is entirely certain where the brain is concerned) but the best guess is to do with energy efficiency; and this is very important for us.

You see, the brain uses a huge amount of energy. We really didn't need it in our earlier evolutionary stages - eating berries and fruits and living a fairly easy working day is a far cry from doing calculus. But the development of the brain allowed us to communicate, to think, to imagine and, as a result, to plan. Doing so allowed us to work in groups and overcome our puny size and strength. We couldn't survive going one-to-one with a mammoth, but working and planning as a group, with weapons we've designed, we could scare whole herds over the edges of cliffs and so feed ourselves during the winter months with ease. But we had to eat more to get more energy to the brain. It's hard to engage in thinking - that's why you get tired in classes, lectures, after studying, or even from just reading a book which you find a bit complex and requires you to concentrate.

Our brains grew, we could do more, technologically advance more, but we needed more food and sometimes that wasn't easy to obtain. There was a trade-off at some point and our brains shrunk to the size they are now and that seemed to be just the right fit. Of course, that didn't happen overnight. It took 200,000 years of growing and then shrinking to this current size.

Why do our brains need so much energy? It's because of how our brain cells (called neurons) work.

There are around 100 billion different neuron cells in your brain and in any particular region there can be around 1000 different neuron types. Even cells which have the same function can have a variety of different shapes and neurologists often give them pretty names like 'chandelier, 'arcade' and 'horse-tail'. To look inside a brain (and yes, we really can do that now) you see what appears to be a tangled jungle of neurons interweaving and wrapping around each other in a seemingly chaotic fashion. But in reality, each of these cells has a specific function and they are needed. It's a highly ordered system - albeit a very complex one.

These neurons typically contain a nucleus, which holds our DNA - the blueprint of what we are - and the 'computer' in every cell in our body which tells the cells which proteins to make and generally what to do. Each neuron has little twig-like spindles sticking out of it called dendrites. How many of these, how long they are (though they are usually short) and how many more 'twigs' branch out of each dendrite varies hugely from neuron to neuron, but these dendrites are the 'input' wires to the neuron. There's also an 'output' wire called an axon. Usually neurons only have one axon, but it can stretch far (even a metre or more) and, like the dendrites, may break off into little 'twigs' to connect to the dendrites of other neurons.

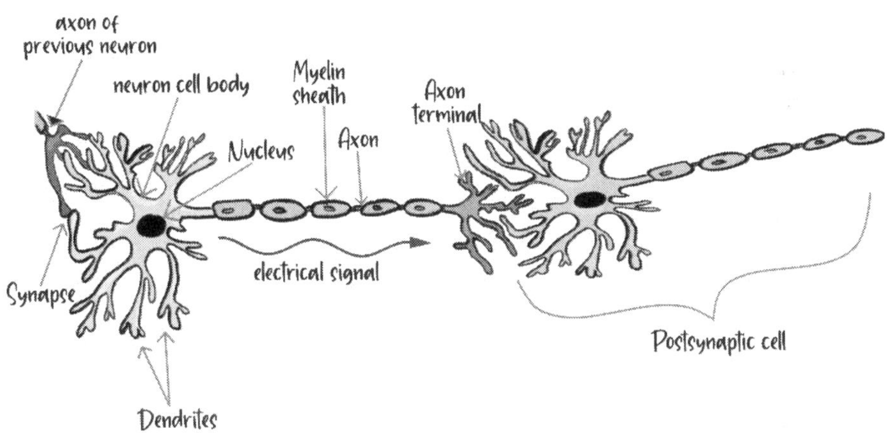

Neurons, axons, dendrites and synapses

In theory, every thought and everything you see, taste, touch, hear and smell makes the axons connect to dendrites to make what's called a 'synapse' - a memory. The truth is far more complicated than that though. A neuron may receive a large number of electrical signals from its dendrites as a result of axons making connections, but only when there's enough signal altogether will the neuron 'fire' its own axon and send a signal on. Worse, some dendrites - called inhibitory - dampen the signal while others - called excitatory - increase the signal. This will be important, as you'll see in a moment.

The connection between an axon and a dendrite is known as a synapse and, strangely, the two parts don't actually touch - they just get very, very close. When an axon is excited it releases charged particles, which are ions known as 'neurotransmitters' and these interact with the surface of the dendrites to cause other ions to move - either in, or out. Ions are charged atoms which have either lost electrons or gained them. Typically sodium or potassium ions, their movement is the chemical equivalent of electricity. In this sense, our brains are electrically active all the time (even when sleeping - actually even more so when sleeping!). Movement takes energy and you don't get this energy for free. Literally millions or billions of synapses are firing neurotransmitters all the time in your brain and that all adds up. That's why you get hungry, your head hurts and you get tired when it has been a long hard day at school or college or wherever you're doing a lot of thinking.

Currently, we think that memory is stored in or controlled by an area of the brain called the hippocampus. You have two of these, one on each side of the brain, low down and not far from where the spinal cord joins. Each is around 3 cm^3. The name 'hippocampus' comes from the Greek words meaning 'horse' and 'sea monster' - in other words, a seahorse, which this part of the brain looks like (a little).

There is debate about exactly how the hippocampus works with memory but, at the very least, it seems to control memory stored around the brain rather than necessarily store all our memories. It also seems to have some influence on the transfer or information going from short-term memory (which is temporary) to long-term memory (which is permanent), although later I will debate whether or not this idea of binary transfer is accurate at all.

Cells in the brain roughly break into two groups. The 'grey matter' is made up of nerve cells and houses these neurons which do the processing of information; and the 'white matter' which is made up of fibres which helps different areas of the brain to communicate together, at least in part by acting as a kind of 'stringy' scaffolding. It is these two types of cell working together which allows us to remember anything at all.

A famous research case looking at cab drivers in London and comparing them to ordinary non-cab drivers identified that their hippocampi were larger than average, which seemed linked to their ability to learn 'The Knowledge' - internalising the London map so they can navigate 25,000 streets from memory. Very specifically, those who qualified as cab drivers had more 'grey matter' in their hippocampus.

It is the mindbogglingly large number of ways our neurons can connect with one another that creates memory. If the idea of electrical signals passing down fibres seems very strangely distant from how we can remember our grandparents when we were kids, or how much we love our pets, or our first kiss or whatever, just remember that computers do the same thing simply by having lots and lots of 'bytes' which can either be 'on' or 'off'. This on/off system (using binary code - a number system entirely made up of zeros and ones) is the way all computer memory is built. These days, that is a pretty impressive computing power and it is getting better every year. Every video you watch, every photo you see, every game you play on your computer or phone - they're all made up of combinations of these little on/off 'switches'. But even the most powerful computer isn't a patch on the humblest human brain. Each neuron could have up to 10,000 connections from other neurons, making a thousand trillion synaptic connections with multiple types of neurotransmitter signals. It's an amazing thing, the brain!

But unlike a computer, we have to create these neuron paths. This is probably where this hippocampus is important again. It is currently thought that new information is channelled there and new neurons made to begin making a 'neural pathway' - in other words, *a memory!*

Learning is an active process, not a passive one. You have to expend energy right from the beginning - from birth - to learn. This is known as 'Action Perception' and a well-known experiment demonstrating this involved two young twin cats which were put in baskets, connected to a system of pulleys. One cat had holes in the basket to enable its legs to make it move. The other cat had no holes in its basket and so couldn't move itself. But when the first cat moved itself around, the pulley system meant that the other cat was moved around too, passively.

When these cats were eventually released, the cat which had been able to move itself around perceived the world perfectly normally. The passive cat, however, could not. Despite having fully functioning sight, it moved as though blind - bumping into walls and so on. It could not 'see' properly and remained that way for the rest of its life. Active involvement in learning from birth about the external world was vital for the cats to be able to perceive the world correctly.

Scientists are still theorizing around how and why memory works but what is clear is that we have to actively engage in the learning process. Just as exercising will increase your muscles and make them more effective, so memorising will strengthen the connections between neurons. An axon that repeatedly fires across a synapse and excites the dendrite will, eventually, result in a greater excitation of that dendrite, making the memory more secure.

Another aspect of learning is that dendrites are 'spiny' - that is, they look like little thin cactuses with even thinner spines sticking out of them. These spines are constantly being formed and then dissolving away and these formations can last minutes, hours, days - or even become permanent. It is thought that these spines are forming to make synapses with nearby axons. If this is so, then it can go quite some way to trashing the idea of fixed short-term and long-term memory. Actually, it's all much more fluid than that and it is about the regular firing of these synapses to make the dendritic spines secure.

One area that researchers are beginning to appreciate in a new way is the role of the myelin sheath. Looking back at the diagram of the neurons, you'll see that the axon is covered in this sheath, which is a kind of fatty, insulating covering which helps keep the axon together.

It has been known for quite a while that the thickness of myelin plays a role in movement, but recent research shows that it plays a role in memory longevity too. In a way, this shouldn't be a surprise. It's a little like the plastic covering of an electrical wire. Not only does that keep you safe from shock (and from electricity taking short cuts through surroundings) but the sheath also keeps the wire together and stops it disintegrating. The same with our neurons. The thicker the myelin sheath, the more stable and persistent the synaptic connection and so the more solid the memory.

All of this takes energy. That's why studying can often seem so tiring (if you've never found yourself falling asleep in classes then you're a lucky person - I have always found it hard work!). Memorising is hard work - it has to be - it is a physical process. That's quite a strange thing for us to get our heads around (pun intended). We take our minds for granted as just 'being there', but they're not. Every thought you have is a chemical process requiring energy.

But why aren't all memories the same? How come I remember my name (usually...) but can't recall where I put my keys?

Theories of memory

"Your mind is like a muscle; the more you use it, the more it grows." (Dr Carol Dweck, Mindset, 2006)

From here on it gets a bit theoretical and uncertain, so I'm not going to go into details about 'episodic' and 'semantic' memory and things like that. Here's the basics which you really need to know.

We have, very clearly and certainly, a short-term memory (STM). Well...sort of certainly, anyway. Arguments continue over the nature and reasons for STM but popular theory says that STM only lasts around 15-30 seconds. It's a little like the RAM in your computer. RAM is a memory place used to allow programs to run but as soon as you turn the computer off, it's all gone. Nothing is stored permanently.

STM is like that. Temporary memory store which allows you to function without instantly forgetting what it was you were doing but the memories are not permanently stored.

Long-term memory (LTM) is stored, obviously from the name, long-term. But that doesn't mean it is necessarily permanent. There are all sorts of things which can get in the way. Neurologically, it does mean that a neural pathway is created and so the memory has a physical place in the brain. Sometimes the memory is stored long-term but our recall lets us down. One theory for why this happens is exactly the same as the one I will say more on later about our brains being wired to forget - that we would be overloaded with information every single day if we recalled everything. Our brains prioritise what's important to recall and what can be allowed to slip away. That way, we can cope with everything we have to deal with each day and only retain what's left. So, sometimes, what was stored in long-term memory can, with disuse, end up forgotten. Or is it?

Personally, I'm not convinced that memory is as cut and dried as traditional psychology theorists want to suggest. We've all experienced times where we've remembered something for longer than 30 seconds. Indeed, I can recall what I ate this morning for my breakfast in quite some detail and that was several hours ago. But I won't remember it next week - or any of the thousands of breakfasts I've had over the years. Except for some special ones - those I can recall very well. For some reason...

Sometimes, when our memory is 'jogged' we can recall something we had 'forgotten' long ago. Of course, it was still stored there in our brains, but we had just lost how to access it. We needed something else to 'jump start' our memory. It's that jump-starting which this book is all about.

Personally, I am quite convinced that memory is on a continuum - from STM to LTM. The key is how well we build those neural paths. Just like our bodies need physical exercise to stay strong and healthy, so our memories have to be exercised. Remember, every memory is a physical connection in your brain and the more you exercise them (or 'activate' them, in science parlance) the more you strengthen them.

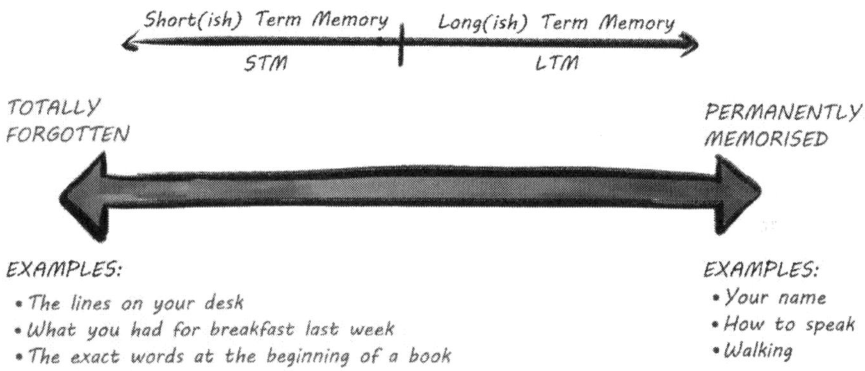

The Memory Continuum

In other words, the more you think about those memories, the more you keep those memories, and the easier it is to 'bring them to mind' when you need to.

Fuzzy Trace, false memories and imagination

A super book I recommend if you become as fascinated about the mind as much as I, is Dr Julia Shaw's *The Memory Illusion.* In this book she talks about something called 'fuzzy trace' theory which basically proposes that, when we remember events, we do so in two different kind of ways simultaneously. The first is a 'fuzzy' memory, the gist of the event – like recalling what topic you were talking about with a friend. The second is the detail, the 'verbatim trace' Shaw calls it, which is the specific details of event – like the very words of the conversation with your friend. Both kinds of memory-building are going on at the same time, according the theory, but I think that's wrong despite the fact it coincides with our lived experience. We all know we can recall the 'general' sense of something that happened *or* the real details. So why do I think it is wrong?

Physiologically, memory is a physical, particular thing. Research has made very clear that neurons are made to react to specific sensations. There are neurons in your brain to hear an A played on a flute which won't react if it is a D# instead. There are neurons which recognise a black stripe moving downwards but won't fire if it moves sideways instead. The millions of neurons are wired to react to every conceivable experience. The 'details' of a memory then are absolutely nailed down by the creation of new synaptic links. So far so good.

But rather than think there's some other 'bigger picture' memorising also going on for the 'gist', I think this is down to the networking nature of our neural connections. It isn't a case of one neuron firing to one neuron. It's each neuron potentially firing to many neurons which, themselves, then fire to many others. It's a huge and complex forest of connections in every part of your brain.

This means that when forming a new memory, you're not just creating an isolated connection in your brain: you're linking to multiple connections. If you meet with a friend for a coffee in a café, it isn't just that memory you're making. The café connects with what you know of cafes. The time with your friend adds to the memories of other times with the same friend. The taste of the coffee adds to your store of coffee tastes. And so on.

The problem with this is that, not only do our brains make these connections with real events, they also make them with imagined ones too. Indeed, this is the premise of Dr Shaw's book. She's famous for actually implanting *false* memories in people's heads (all in the name of good science, of course). The problem is that with so much networking going on, it is easy for things to get confused. You can recall your conversation with your friend in great detail (verbatim trace) but you've got completely the wrong café in your head. You've done this, admit it. We all have.

While that's bad news for reliable witnesses and legal proceedings, it is *good news* for us. The fact that imagination can be tapped into and used to make strong memories is going to be absolutely key for the system you'll learn in Chapter Four.

The problem with traditional ways of memorising

The thought of exercising memories mentioned earlier, leads us on to some of the issues with traditional ways of memorising and why you need this book.

The 'industry standard' advice for cramming for tests and exams is this: revise, revise, revise. Or, to put it another way: go over the same information again and again. In Asian countries - particularly those who were ruled by the British during the Colonial era - this has taken on a hideous form. In many places, like Bangladesh (where I taught for many years), students effectively 'learn by rote'. It starts at a young age where many children are expected to memorise poems and recite them 'word perfect' in front of the teacher, their classmates or perhaps in front of larger audiences at special school occasions.

This is reminiscent of the days where children in British schools were expected to learn whole passages from Shakespeare to recite publicly. While this is all very impressive and can, of course, move audiences greatly if performed well, most schools no longer do this in the West because it is not a skill we especially value any longer. The work needed for such memorisation puts unnecessary pressure on students, most of whom cannot manage such gargantuan tasks with any ease. While Western education has moved on, old colonial countries have tended to remain with what used to be perceived 'good practice'. The traditional perception remains that if you can't recite from memory then you haven't learnt it yet.

Today, millions of students spend (I would say 'waste') countless hours memorising information 'by rote' without necessarily truly understanding what they are learning. Why does this practice of 'rote learning' continue? Because, in the end, it works! For the reasons I stated earlier, if you keep 'activating the memory' then you will strengthen it and be more likely to recall it in an exam.

But 'rote learning' is not an *effective* way to learn. If you are spending hours writing out, or speaking out, the same information over and over again, you're not spending that time learning other things or consolidating your understanding. Indeed, many students worldwide struggle with - or even fail - exams because they spent so long trying to cram facts into their heads that they don't really understand what it is they've shoved in there and can't use that information well when asked questions testing their comprehension. I've known this to be the case from 12-year-olds doing a history test, mangling periods of history together, through to medical students who can list perfectly a dozen possible issues that may be wrong with a patient but have no idea how to assess which one is most likely to be correct to use for treatment.

In fact, memories are formed very quickly and don't need that much time to establish them. The trick is to master the recall. Get that sorted and you can speed through a lot more and be more certain of your memory in the exam. This fact is well known to all the 'grand masters' of memory skills and is the core to all mnemonics books like this one. Have a system for recall which works and you can concentrate on 'exercising' your memory to make it strong, quickly and efficiently.

Rote learning is the making of new neurons and reinforcing them by repetition. This is how we learned to walk and talk. It takes time. Mnemonics is the hotwiring of the brain through using images and ideas *ALREADY PRESENT* in the brain and making very few new connections to speed up the process of making permanent - or semi-permanent - memories. The more energy used in making the connection, the faster a more permanent synaptic link will form.

If memory then, is a physical thing. It stands to reason that you need a body which is working well. The next chapter looks at this very idea and gives you advice on making sure you're physically ready for the work ahead.

However, even though the brain is a remarkable piece of biological machinery, there's an issue. Every single day it is dealing with millions of bits of information. Look around you right now. What do you see? Don't just look at the normal stuff but notice the details. I'm at my desk and I can see a ton of books, nearly as many unopened letters and other paperwork, my laptop and monitor plus a few other bits and pieces. That's straightforward, but I've neglected to mention the grains in the wood of my bookshelves or on the desk itself. There's one, two, three, four...no, I'm just not going to be able to tell you how many different lines there are running along each shelf. It's just too many. And yet I can see them all - and if I can see it, then my brain has decoded it internally. In theory, thousands of data from just sitting at my desk are logged in my brain. Think how many more there are for every room I go to, every place I see, every person I meet.

So how come I won't remember most of it? Not even a fraction. What's going on?

The Art of Forgetting

By useful coincidence, just as I was about to begin this chapter, a former student of mine got in touch. She's taking a degree in Law and has just taken her first exam. It went well, I'm pleased to say, but she told me how she berated herself for forgetting some details.

"There were some trial court cases I knew I knew," she told me, "but because I was nervous, they just went straight out of my head!"

She had forgotten to use techniques I had taught her many years before - easily done when you get out of the habit of memorising. My former student had assumed that because she knew these cases so well it would be impossible for her to forget them in an exam. She hadn't allowed for the effect nervousness and pressure have on our memory.

In fact, there are many things which can affect our memory: sleep, food, health, stress, alcohol, tea & coffee, other drugs and stimulants…the list goes on. We take this powerhouse of our body we call the brain for granted so much that we forget that it isn't just the brain which affects the body but the other way around too. Remember, those ions I mentioned earlier are just chemicals. If you don't have enough of those chemicals, then synapses can't fire and memories don't stick. Where do you get these chemicals? From everything you eat, drink and breathe in.

I recall, soon after my daughter was born, completely forgetting her name when I was at a social event after a stranger asked me. It was excruciatingly embarrassing! How can a new father forget the name of his first child? Very easily, believe me, when said child doesn't sleep well at night and both parents are dreadfully sleep-deprived! During those first few months of parenthood I messed up plenty of times including, for a few seconds, forgetting my own name when introducing myself to someone. Now my memory is bad, but it isn't that bad! It was simply a combination of lack of sleep and the stress of meeting someone new.

It's not just something as understandable as sleep deprivation when you have a baby that causes memory loss (albeit temporarily).

Just recently, I was walking my dog. She's a beautiful, happy, friendly animal and is a Cocker Spaniel breed. Cocker Spaniels are all gorgeous and attract strangers in the streets like jam draws wasps. This particular time, it was a group of guys coming out of a pub and looking just slightly tipsy. One took a shine to my dog (who loved the attention, of course) and he asked me what breed she was.

"Oh," said I, "she's a Border Collie."

If you know anything about dog breeds you'll know that Cocker Spaniels and Border Collies look nothing alike. They're not the same size, the same colour, temperament or anything. Apart from having a nose, four legs, fur and a tail, these are totally different creatures. Thankfully, the guy was slightly worse for wear and he just said, "Oh right, cool" and wandered off. I was mortified.

So now I use a memory aid (just a key word/image - don't ask what it is but if you're British you might be able to guess) which means I'll never make that mistake again. I'm ready for the next time someone asks me what kind of dog I have!

But why did I forget her breed? I have certificates of lineage for her and everything, so I know very well what kind of dog she is. Why did I forget? I don't really know - other than I was suddenly asked a question from a stranger I wasn't expecting. It was enough to scramble my brain cells like people rushing in a store, panic-buying on the first day of January sales - my head was all over the place! Fear, tiredness, ill health...they all can hinder memory. There's so many things working against us when it comes to exams.

My student friend had forgotten the impact being nervous has on memory and had no way to be able to claw back those case names which had just left her head. I gave her a fast refresher course on memory aids (took minutes to write in a text and just seconds for her to read and understand). A week later she took another test and remembered all the case study names. It really is that simple once you're used to using the techniques in this book.

The moral of the story is this:

Don't assume just because you know something really, really well, that you will remember it when under fire and you have. You need a back-up plan.

I don't know how old you are or how good you think your memory is normally but there's a good chance you have encountered the situation known to almost all of us where you've lost something vital just as you need to go out somewhere. It might be your house keys or your phone or the birthday present you had ready ages ago for the party you're now going to and you put it in a 'safe place'. Now you can't find the blooming thing anywhere! You hunt high and low for it but no matter where you look, you can't find it.

If you're lucky, you come across it just in the nick of time, other times, you have to go without, but you find it the next day with ease. Inevitably, when you locate it you have the 'ohhhh yeah...' moment where it all comes back to you just where you were and why you put it where you did. I'm pretty sure that our cavemen ancestors had the same issue, banging around the caves trying to find their flint weapons in time for a hunting raid.

The problem here isn't with memory: It's with recall.

Usually when we say we've forgotten something, really what's happening is that we can't recall it properly. Once something triggers the recall (far too often it's looking at your revision notes after the exam) we tend to slap our heads and go, "Of course! I knew that!". It all comes back to us. We remember the information, we remember why we put our keys down in that room and what we were doing at the time, and we remember why we thought that obscure place was a really good place to put the present.

Why is it that we have this whole 'recall' thing at all? Why can't we just remember stuff and it sticks forever? Here's the secret reason why:

Our brains are designed to forget.

Let that sink in.

Yes, our brains are this amazing set of neurons wired together to organise everything from making all our organs work together to remember how to walk and where we put our phone. But the brain also deliberately does a huge amount of forgetting. Why? For exactly the reason I've stated earlier on: we take in a massive amount of information all the time. If the brain was remembering all this stuff we'd expend a ridiculous amount of energy to keep it all in and anything we actually needed to remember would be swamped with millions of trivial pieces of data like how many spots of fluff were on your coat last August 20th and things like that. Indeed, there are a few people (very few – evolution has decided this is a bad trait and done its best to eliminate it) who don't forget the things they see. Almost all of them see it as a curse. For some, it is autobiographical information: they can remember every day of their lives. For others, often on the autistic spectrum, it is amazing abilities at specific skills and specific kinds of information. Usually, such people struggle with many aspects of everyday life.

The fact is, you can't have it both ways – functional life *and* super-charged memory. It just isn't efficient to remember everything. The brain has to decide what to just chuck away, what to keep, what to store - but it then requires you to remember the password to access it (in other words, recall).

The way around this is to 'hotwire' your brain. Or, to put it another way - make organised use of your brain. Help it know what needs keeping and what needs throwing out: train your recall. This needs a system which will make you concentrate in very specific ways to make the connections. Attention (or concentration) is the muscle of memory. You remember those emotion-filled moments the best because you gave them the attention they need. Attention takes energy and energy is the pay-off for memory.

Recall is the trick to having a good, reliable memory. This book is going to give you the resources to make sure you can recall whatever you've memorised and never have to worry about getting nervous again.

EXERCISE:

How much of that nonsense story can you recall? Have a go now, before moving on, to see how much of it you remember. Flick back to the start of the chapter and see how you did. Was there anything you forgot?

I promised you that, despite the nonsense of the story, you had actually memorised something very real. We will look at exactly what was going on with this story later in chapter four, but for now, I'll tell you what you memorised:

The Solar System.

Yep. You did. You now know the order of the planets from the Sun. Here's how…

Firstly, you pictured a boy. That was somebody's *son* which sounds like *Sun*. He was playing with silver balls. *Mercury* is a silver-coloured liquid. The beautiful woman was *Venus,* the Roman goddess of love and associated with beauty. She threw the balls into the ground throwing up *Earth* all over the place which then got the 'angry, red-faced and small' neighbour furious – a perfect description of the planet *Mars* and its associated Roman god of war. He was crushed by the Roman god of all gods – *Jupiter*. And on Jupiter's shirt was the word SUN, very conveniently giving us a linked word, the letters of which give an acronym for *Saturn, Uranus, Neptune.* And just for free, despite no longer being considered a planet (though it was in my day, as a kid), I've given you the famous cartoon dog, *Pluto*!

You will need to have some prior knowledge to make that simple memory story useful – knowing some Roman gods and being aware of the properties of mercury – but that point was made earlier. When memorising, it is important you understand the material you're trying to memorise. Nevertheless, even if you knew none of this, you still remembered that story, right? That's the beauty of this system!

Chapter 3 – Preparing the ground

"Tell me what you eat and I will tell you what you are." Anthelme Brillat-Savarin.

I remember being young fondly. Really fondly...sigh...

Back then I could burn the candle at both ends, staying up till the early hours of the morning, then getting up for lessons at the crack of dawn, eating and drinking whatever I wished - remaining thin as a stick while I consumed everything - and somehow not just surviving it but actually thriving. Long gone are those days.

In my old(er) age now, I struggle to stay up later than 9pm, feel decidedly ill if I get less than six hours sleep each night and if I just look at a burger or a cream cake I can feel my arteries tighten and my tummy bulge. These days I know the importance of diet, exercise and generally trying to keep a healthy lifestyle. Very few young people do, and I don't blame them. You're invincible when young!

From an evolutionary point of view, this is quite correct. When we were living in caves with sabre-tooth tigers out for a 'man-sized snack', you needed youth and energy on your side - the ability to do an awful lot for a long time and survive it. You'd eat like crazy to store energy and your body could roll with the punches for as long as needed to make sure you and your clan remained safe.

The twin problems of today however are that our diets were much better back then, and we don't go around strenuously battling large man-eating cats. Not often, anyway. Instead, we call on our youth to sit down for hours on end, studying, revising and learning. Then we expect them to regurgitate all this in the exam hall, year after year. At one point in the UK, it was estimated that children go through more than 80 hours of tests and exams by the time they are sixteen. That's a crazy amount when you think of it, but not uncommon around the world.

And here's the thing - your brain is a massive energy consumer. When you eat and drink you are, in a very large part, literally feeding your brain. So the first thing you need to do, in preparing the ground for a good, efficient memory, is to make sure you are eating and drinking right. This section actually goes way beyond that. If you set yourself up right now, you'll gain good nutritional habits which will continue on for the rest of your life.

This is important for the reasons alluded to a moment ago. If you're young (around 13-25) then the chances are, you feel like you can just keep going and what you eat and drink doesn't matter that much. At my age, I can physically *feel* when I've eaten or drunk things which aren't good for you, or if I've not eaten enough of the nutrients I *do* need. My stamina flags by midday if I've not eaten the right things or drunk enough water. Our bodies' needs aren't different, just the ability to cope with things for longer has changed. You still need all those nutrients to keep your brain working at top level, whether you feel like it or not. And one day, you *will* feel it. So, develop these habits now. The good news: this is all food which is good for you in general and there's plenty of options and alternatives to find things you like. No one is going to be force-feeding you Brussel sprouts or mushrooms.

Brain Food & Drink

You need to make sure you have a balanced diet but bear in mind that I am just looking at food which is helpful to make your brain work at optimum levels. This is *not* a comprehensive list and if you have allergies or any other medical issues you should, of course, consult a doctor. So don't go try to live on nuts and fish alone or anything. Our bodies use a staggering range of chemical elements arranged together in a bewildering array of proteins, amino acids and whatnot.

The less balanced a diet you have, the less balanced your body will be. It really is that simple!

Here then is a list of good stuff to eat or drink with a very short summary of why. I'm not going to go into details about all the chemicals involved and the physiology of it all. Just enough to explain why you should eat as much from this list as you can.

Fish – arguably the educationalist's go-to food because of the famous Omega-3 oils with reputed almost magical results on improving memory and learning in children. Some of these results have been a little debunked over the years but, nevertheless, fish oils are good for you. Your brain is substantially made up of fat with half of it being the Omega-3 kind. This fat is necessary to keep the structure in the brain, building the membranes around cells - the result is better memory and cognition skills. Almost any fish is going to be good but recommended types include tuna, sardines, herring and salmon. If fish doesn't do it for you, soya beans, pumpkin seeds and walnuts are fine alternatives.

Eggs – in some ways, the king of all foods which are good for you, eggs have a ton of useful nutrients including B6 and B12 vitamins. Eggs help regulate mood and help the neurotransmitters involved in memory. Alternative sources of B12 include breakfast cereals and plant milks while for B6 there's avocado, soya and nuts or seeds. In general, chicken, fish and leafy greens are good for the B stuff.

Broccoli – I hated this stuff when I was a kid but have grown to love it as the years have gone by. Just as well! There's lots of vitamin K which is essential for a type of fat so necessary in the brain. This food helps the breakdown of neurotransmitters - and don't forget, without those, you get no memory - so, eat this stuff. Not bad for Vitamin C too.

Wholegrains – say what? This is basically a load of food stuffs like cereals, brown rice, pasta and granary bread which are a good source of carbohydrates. Carbohydrates are the 'good' source of sugar we need which gives us energy. I don't just mean at the 'can I be bothered to get out of bed' energy. I mean, at a cellular level and, as you know now, memory is all about cellular activity. You need those carbs to keep your brain firing and stop it being sluggish.

Seeds and nuts – When I was a kid there was no way I'd have eaten seeds. I had visions of plants growing out of my stomach and stuff. Turns out, I was wrong. Not only are roasted seeds delicious but they are full of things like zinc, magnesium, copper and iron which all do important jobs in the brain, most noticeably, allowing you to think clearly. Nuts have also been linked to giving people sharper memories. There's a ridiculous amount of good stuff in nuts – healthy fats, Vitamin E, etc – which make them a super choice; *if* you're not allergic to them. Pumpkin seeds are very good, as are sunflower seeds (my favourite). Walnuts, almonds, peanuts and hazelnuts are excellent too. If you can't bear the idea of seeds growing plants inside you (again, they don't, really) then beef, oysters (like who can afford those?), asparagus, olives, brown rice, wholegrains and chickpeas are good to go as alternatives.

Oil – seeds and nuts can be crushed and their oils extracted. As you now know, certain oils (unsaturated, if you must know) are really good for you and your brain. Olive oils (extra virgin especially) are super. If you cook for yourself, go for good oil to cook with. If not, check with the cook of your house and see what they use. Beware, too much oil in cooking is really bad for you, whatever kind you use; but a small amount, regularly, is very good indeed.

Berries – many experts claim that blueberries are the very best berries to eat if you care about your brain. Personally, I find them a bit yucky but luckily other berries are just as good really. There's some evidence to suggest they improve short term memory, allow neurons to communicate better and relieve stress. Strawberries are also great too with lots of vitamin C to boot. Dark fruits like blackberries, blackcurrants and vegetables like red cabbage are good alternatives too.

Fruit – oranges are well known for their famous vitamin C content which is a key nutrient for preventing mental decline. Kiwi fruit is also good for this, as are peppers, blackcurrents and tomatoes. Bananas are a fruit I've recommended to students for years to eat before exams. Bananas are rich in potassium (good for synapses) and are a good source of sugar but with the added benefit of plenty of fibre which helps slow down the digestion of that sugar. The result: a slow-release stimulant. Research has shown eating bananas before a long bike ride helps endurance and performance. They will help you keep your energy up in exams too, but they are good to eat regularly in general, if you can.

Turmeric – perhaps the unrealised magic spice that my Asian friends may never have realised was so important? The lovely yellow spice so beloved in curries, it turns out, can ease depression, helps new brain cells to grow and possibly helps improve memory.

Dark chocolate – much though I'm wary of suggesting chocolate as a healthy food, *dark* chocolate (not milk or white) does have some brain benefits and has been linked to improving the plasticity of the brain (meaning the ability to form new neural connections). It enhances brain skills involving memory and mental tasks and helps slow down age-related mental decline (hmm...maybe I need some of this stuff myself?). It is also a well-known mood improver so makes it a great stimulant to eat before tackling revision if you're feeling a bit down in the dumps.

Coffee – personally, I can't stand the stuff *but* there's no doubt that this drink is a remarkable stimulant for the brain. I once had a student who could barely add 2 + 2 in our maths lessons but if she had a coffee beforehand was virtually a mathematical genius. And while I wrote that sentence for dramatic effect, I'm only *slightly* exaggerating in both directions. Coffee had an astounding effect. If you drink this stuff already, then targeted drinking before exams and when undertaking solid revision work is an excellent idea.

Green tea – ah, this is more like it. None of that yucky coffee stuff – *tea* is the bee's knees! However, not normal so-called 'builder's tea'. Green tea (also known as Jasmine tea or Chinese tea) is brilliant for improving memory, focus and alertness. Green tea also relaxes you and calms anxiety – very important the night before exams!

Water – it should hardly need saying really that keeping hydrated is essential for good health. The brain is no different. Water is involved in every cell in your body and is essential for life. I'm pleased to have seen, over my lifetime, a change in attitudes to water in the classroom. When I was a kid, getting a water bottle out in class would have led to a detention. By the time I was Deputy Head of department in a UK West Cumbrian school in the early 2000s, every student had a bottle of water on their desk and no one thought twice about it. Water helps deliver nutrients to your brain and takes away toxins. Fully hydrated, you will think faster, more creatively and focus better too.

So that's my list. It's not exhaustive, but hopefully much of what's on here you already eat. The trick is to be consistent and regular. Choose which foods you like best and make sure you eat them often. Try adding in some things you wouldn't normally eat. For instance, until around twelve years ago, I had eggs and nuts only from time to time despite loving both. For some reason, nuts were always a 'Christmas treat' when I was growing up, and as an adult I rarely thought of them except for that holiday season. Now I eat nuts every day and feel so much healthier for it. And in the mornings, it is rare I don't either eat banana or an egg or two. I have really felt the difference in my ability to concentrate, learn and remember things.

Physical Exercise

Just as you are what you eat, so you become what you exercise. Again, youthfulness is the enemy of common sense. When young you have an almost boundless amount of energy and strength to leap into action when the spirit so moves, seemingly without preparation and often on a diet the nutritional equivalent of dry cardboard. But that automatically limits what you can achieve, even when it doesn't feel like it; and it is only when you're older that you start to appreciate why it would have been a good idea to exercise more when younger.

Today, I exercise at least three times a week, sometimes every day, and have hugely improved my physical ability – but at the same time, my body is more easily damaged, more susceptible to illness and, generally, finds it harder to improve. I have the strange situation of being both the healthiest I've ever been (it's not a high bar to get over, truth be told) and continuing the daily fight of preventing my body falling apart. I certainly rue not making the effort to get fit earlier in life.

So, not only is it just a good idea generally, but exercise is also good for your brain too. Just as in Part II we'll see how exercising your brain is important when it comes to making memories permanent, so exercising your body is important for the physical shape of your mind. Exercise helps your overall mood and your ability to think, problem solve and recall memories.

Exercise doesn't need to be hard. I'm not talking about swimming 40 laps a day or lifting heavy weights. Going for a walk is a great form of exercise. Indeed, as you'll see, the memory story system means that you don't need to write anything down you don't wish to and you can actually be working on your revision *while* walking – killing two birds with one stone, as they say. However, the more taxing your aerobic or cardio exercise you can do, the better. If you walk, walk briskly. Running, cycling and swimming are good too if you do enjoy these activities. This kind of exercise helps increase the size of your hippocampus and that, if you can recall from the previous chapter, is good for your memory.

Your body does reward you for exercising, releasing hormones which make you feel happy. It's one of the oddities in life that often the thought of making yourself exercise can be the opposite! Your brain likes to conserve energy and so tends to push you to do as little as possible. But at the same time, it knows exercise is good for you *for the future,* and so once you've done some exercise, it tells you that you did good.

From our point of view, exercise is good because studying is often boring. When that happens, your brain starts to turn off. Studies have shown that concentration spans today can be as short as 20 minutes. While there's no harm learning to push that and build up your stamina for study, nevertheless, it makes sense to work within your strengths. There's no point trying to study for an hour if you actually spend 40 minutes just staring at your notes with nothing going in. Getting up and going for a 10-minute walk gets your mind active again and gives you renewed energy and interest. It's worth investing in that time if it means you don't have any wasted study time as a result.

Sleep

This area should almost be a slam-dunk, no-brainer, and as such I will not spend much time on it. That said, sleep is one of those annoying parts of our life which scientists have researched a ridiculous amount and yet still shuffle their feet when asked that most basic of questions: *why do we sleep?*

I could tell you lots about what researchers *do* know about sleep, and all the fascinating aspects of the various levels of sleep we go through each night, but I won't. The bottom line, that you need to know right now is this: sleep is really, really important – even if we don't really know why.

Sleep deprivation studies have shown us what happens when we don't get enough sleep, but if you've ever pulled an 'all-nighter', or even just had one of those awful nights where you just can't sleep, you'll know just how like death you feel when it comes to the next day.

The key trick is to figure out how much sleep you need and stick pretty close to it. If you get too little, you'll struggle to concentrate, to give attention and, as a result, to keep things in your memory. If you get too much, there's a good chance you'll find yourself suffering insomnia as your body's sleep cycle goes all out of sync with itself. The result is that you'll end up having less sleep and a sleep routine which is a disaster.

Most people need around 6-8 hours sleep per night. Try to figure out for yourself where you fit on this scale. It is tempting, especially when young, to ignore this. We've all done the 'burning the candle at both ends' way of living when young. Trust me: in the end it really screws with you.

I personally need to sleep around 6-7 hours. For many, many years I suffered dreadful insomnia, brought on by a screwed body clock. As a child, I was 'made' to go to bed at a prescribed time whether I was tired or not and inevitably lay awake in the dark for hours and hours, every night. As a teenager I gained freedom from that routine but then saw sleep as a horrid waste of time and was your true academic nerdy night owl, staying up until 2am or more every single night.

Eventually, as an adult with a full-time teaching job, I settled into a routine of staying up late one night to work until around 3am and then the next night going to sleep around usual, reasonable time (10pm-ish) in order to avoid the horrors of lying awake in the dark until around 5am *every* night. I did this late night/early night routine for several years until, eventually, my own body clock altered with age and got used to a slightly longer sleep pattern. These days I need about seven hours per night and I no longer need to have an on/off sleeping arrangement.

It took me literally about forty years to finally get a decent night's sleep – don't make the same mistake. Your brain needs sleep, for whatever reason, in order to function properly. So treat sleep the same way you should for exercise and diet: get it sorted!

Your study area and routine

That leads us nicely onto the final part of preparing the ground for the memory system to come – your environment and your routine.

Where you study is important and you need to be honest with yourself about whether or not you are working in the best way. You might enjoy studying on your bed, but if that makes you sleepy (it does when I used to try it) then it is no good. Conversely, if you sit at your desk with a hard chair, to try and make yourself concentrate, but you get uncomfortable quickly, that's no better!

There's no simple 'do this' rules here. In some cases, you might want to try moving places every 20 minutes or so. Set a timer on your phone perhaps?

Your phone could be another problem. It's one of my great weaknesses, I'll admit. Even as I write this, my phone is just within the range of my peripheral vision. If a message comes, I'll see it and there's a good chance I'll pick it up to look and be distracted for five minutes. When I need to do some solid, concentrated work, I need to turn that phone over and put it out of reach. If you're the same, get it out of the way. Same goes for games consoles, TV remote controls or any other distraction.

Music is a distraction for some too, while being essential work sound for others. I find that music with singing is a disaster. As a musician, I tune into the words way too much and can't concentrate on what I'm trying to do. I often work in silence and I know many people that have to have a silent room to work. But sometimes, ambient sound is helpful. I now regularly use 'Focus music' which is a function on my Amazon Alexa, but in the past I've listened to the sounds of rain, or the beach, or even the sounds of a train journey – all available on the internet – to have background sounds which are peaceful yet somehow help the brain focus.

A more difficult demand is to try and keep your room tidy. There's two reasons for this. Firstly, a messy room is really distracting and can lead you to focus more on the mess than on your study. The second is that it can really help reinforce your memory-making if you get up and move around the room as you're doing it! I'll come back to this in Part II, but remember the cats mentioned in the previous chapter? Memory is an active activity – the more active you make your study, the stronger your memory making will be. You could combine this with getting your phone out of the way perhaps. Put it in the kitchen while you study. When you're done, you'll have to get up and walk to where you left it. Why not get a glass or water or make a cup of green tea while you're at it?

One final point

I've already stated that this book isn't going to teach you your subject material and memorising systems aren't going to help you understand it. I'm going to reiterate this again here because it really is important that, before you start trying to memorise facts, ***you fully understand the material you've been learning.*** If you do – great! – you're good to go and, when you really get the hang of the system, you'll be able to start memorising instantly – in the classroom, from the book, or whatever you're using to learn from.

But if not, then spend time making sure you understand the concepts. There are numerous ways to do this and I would suggest you work through them until you find that 'Eureka' moment when it all clicks into place and you've got it.

- Look up the subject matter on YouTube – it's my go-to resource for anything I don't know or don't understand. You can almost always find 2-10 minute videos explaining pretty much any subject you like. Go for the ones which look slick, have perhaps some animation and, most importantly, have a large number of views. This should safeguard you from the occasional wally out there who thinks they understand Tudor History of Differentiation and really hasn't a clue.

- Ask an expert – which for most of you means asking your teacher! Sometimes, just asking someone to explain something helps to bring the subject to life. There's a lot of forums out there on the internet too which can be helpful. Be careful though, sometimes well-meaning people give inaccurate advice. If someone makes sense, go back to the book or watch a video and check that their advice confers with authorities on the matter.
- Read a book! This might be strange but often the reason people don't understand something is that the lesson, lecture or video class they've just had is the problem. The instructor is confusing or perhaps isn't that great at communicating ideas. If that's the case, go to the textbook. Alternatively, web pages will do the same thing. Wikipedia is good for this though sometimes it goes into confusing detail you don't want. Other pages – like the BBC's Bitesize are great for giving concise, accurate information in very clear ways.
- Read in advance. Related to the last idea, the difference here is that if you find lessons or videos difficult, find out what will be taught next and read the textbook in advance. If you're someone who finds reading really helpful, this can give you a head start for that class, so you're not left playing catch-up.

EXERCISE:

Make a list of everything you eat today. Keep a track of this for the next few days. While you're at it, list down how much time you spend walking or doing other exercise. Also look at your study environment and see how it can be improved. Can you walk around? Do you need to move off your bed? Will timers on your phone help or do you need to put that thing in a drawer while you study? Also do the maths to figure out how many hours of sleep you need and build a routine which doesn't push it out or neglect sleep as important.

Once you've worked on all this for a few days, or a week, start putting into place how you can put together your best environment, exercise routine and diet to give your brain the best physical condition to actually do its work.

And work it shall like never before! That's coming in Part II…

Part II – The Memory Story System

Chapter 4 – Memory stories (or how to memorise stuff)

Now we come to the actual business of memorising stuff. You've already had a taste of what is to come when I gave you the story which turned out to be about the planets. I'm going to make a solid bet that you can still remember most – if not all – of that story now. Why does it work so well?

Human beings – sensory creatures

Evolution has adapted us – and, to be fair, pretty much all life on Earth – to be sensory creatures. That means there's a mechanism giving our very internal brains the ability to have contact with the outside world. This may seem really straightforward and obvious, but it hides something astonishing.

Everything you think you know passes through the filter of your nerves. Sensory neurons are all over your skin, in your eyes, ears, nose, mouth and a few inside your body too (which is how you know you have a stomach ache after too much chocolate pudding). These are your 'senses', traditionally considered sight, hearing, smell, taste and touch, although some experts add a few extra senses into that list. These sensory neurons send signals to the brain, which then interprets them and decides if action is needed in response. If it is, then the brain sends signals through motor neurons to muscles in your body to make them move in some way or another. So, for instance, a light might shine into your eyes, the sensory neuron (your optic nerve at the back of the eye) sends a signal to the brain, the brain decodes the signal (there's a bright light shining) and sends signals through motor neurons to your eyelid muscles (close eyes now!).

But here's the weird thing: this means everything you think you sense about the world is fake.

Everything you touch, taste, hear or see is all interpretation done by your brain. It all depends on your brain's ability to decode the nerve signals and work out what's going on. This is why illusions – all forms of them – are so baffling. Optical illusions are the obvious ones and are very famous. In recent years, the so-called 'dress' illusion has really demonstrated just how much our minds are interpreting things. If you don't know what I'm talking about, go google 'dress illusion' and you'll find it. Some of us see the dress as black and blue and some see it as gold and white. We're each absolutely convinced we're seeing it right. There are auditory illusions as well and sensory too. Magicians make use of this all the time; and I should know – I am one! We set up a scenario which has you thinking in a certain way so that when we do our 'thing' – sleight of hand, misdirection or some other secret something – you're caught off-guard and left unable to work out exactly what happened. Your brain has told you something happened that simply couldn't have, and you are fooled.

Why does this happen? When the brain is making neural connections, it does so constantly for every single piece of sensory information it is receiving. The importance of that information is then evaluated by the connections it makes with other neural networks. This hugely speeds up the process of making sense of the world. If our ancestors looked at something new coming over the horizon and busied themselves with working out all its details and wondering what it was, that might be a disaster. Instead, they look at that something and make the connection that it was 'tiger'-shaped and scarper as fast as they could! We still do that to this day and, again, we can be fooled, especially in the dark. I've woken up before today and been momentarily panicked into thinking there's someone in my room only to discover that it is just my dressing gown hanging on the back of the door. In the pale light of night, my brain has seen the elongated shape and gone "that's man shape – DANGER! Wake up and run!"

Out of all our senses, it is arguably our sight which is most used and honed. This means it is also the ideal sense to hack into to use for memorising. In fact, all our senses make memories – exactly for the aforementioned process of sensory neurons passing information to the brain. When you hear your parents call to you, you recognise their voices – that's a memory. When you pick up your mug from the table without particularly looking, you know you've grabbed the right thing because you recognise the feel – that's a memory. When you enter a shop and smell fresh bread baking and your mouth starts to salivate – that's a memory. So you can, in fact, make memory aids using any or all of the senses. We'll come back to this later, but for now, we're going to base this system firmly around vision. It's our most reliable and well-practised sense.

So highly trained is our vision that we can see things that aren't there – in our imagination. While it is possible to smell food or hear a voice in our heads, these things are actually really quite difficult to do in any real tangible way. I can only vaguely imagine the smell of fresh tomatoes or feel of wood. I'm slightly better at imaging the sound of my parents or children, but even that is a little uncertain. But I can *picture* all those things with ease. That's important.

Many – if not most – mnemonics (memory techniques) rely on getting you to visualise things and this system is no different. We will try to turn everything – including numbers, languages scripts and faces – into objects we can see with ease. There's nothing new in this method, what's more novel is the realisation that we don't just memorise things as separate entities – we make connections with other things. This isn't just the fact that we have a store of 'chair'-like objects or 'house'-like objects or 'big, dangerous man-eating cats'-like objects. We also remember things chronologically. This is why, when you've been somewhere once or twice, you can usually begin to figure out how to get there again. You're able to retrace your steps and work out which corner you turn first, what landmark you pass next and what road you go down third…and so on.

It is this linking of memorable pictures which is going to be the cornerstone of the memory story method. It's why the Planets story worked so well. The images are so strong and easy to see and the connections of one to the other, so straightforward it is hard *not* to see what comes next.

Let's try it again but with a new scenario and for a different purpose.

Memory Story – Let's go shopping!

Unless you're a most unusual person (lazy? Just kidding!), at some point in your life you've probably gone food shopping – with or without someone else, such as a parent or spouse. Let's imagine you've got a list of the following:

Eggs

Bread

Cucumbers

Cheese

Toilet roll

Pasta

Pens

Rice

Deodorant

Toothpaste

Flour

Bananas

That's quite a list (off the top of my head too, deliberately all mixed up). Under normal circumstances you'd be writing this down. If you didn't, and you're quite sure you could remember that list having read it once or heard someone say it to you once, then you don't need this book – your memory is exceptional!

Still here? Good, then you're like me and have a dud mind; except I can remember this list – and pretty flawlessly too – on one run through.

The trick is what I call *'Memory Stories'*. This is where you visualise the things you want to remember and string each one on to another. This stringing together is absolutely vital and is the key aspect to this system. You're not memorising an individual picture as many old traditional methods do – you're memorising a mini-movie. Here's how to do it with this shopping list. Read the next paragraph slowly and visualise each part carefully. Don't skimp on this – it is vital!

You're standing at the entrance of the supermarket or shop you usually do your shopping in. Adapt this story to suit your own shop. You're shaking yourself down after coming in from the rain outside – except it was raining eggs! You're covered in yoke and start to wipe yourself down using slices of bread which are on a table just inside the shop. You realise this is going to get your hands dirty so you start to spear the bread with some cucumbers which have just been handed to you. You pay the man who gave you the cucumbers from your pocket – but you pay him in cheese slices! Weirdly, he accepts and hands you some change – in the form of sheets of toilet paper. The paper is really useful because you use it to scoop up lots of pasta from a bucket and wrap it up in the paper. One long tube of pasta grabs your eye as you pick it up and realise it is a pen! But when you click the end of it from the nib, rice pours out of it instead. You can't stop the rice pouring so you jam the pen into a can of deodorant which starts spraying out of control. You panic, but another shopper comes over happily and picks it up to spray his teeth as though it was toothpaste and starts cleaning his teeth with his toothbrush. To finish off, he rinses his mouth out with…flour! How horrible – even he finds this hard to swallow (literally) so he makes the taste better by grabbing a banana and trying to eat it. But the flour and banana together go all gloopy and his mouth gets stuck. What a strange shopping trip!

If you've paid attention to that story and given yourself a couple of seconds to fix each image in your mind, the chances are you've now got that entirely shopping list memorised in one go. If not, read it again and pay attention to what you missed. You should find once more around will do it. This system works a lot better when you start making your own images to memorise the stuff that is relevant to you, but this quick story gives you a good gist of how easy it is.

Notice how each item links on to the next? The eggs are wiped down by bread. The bread is speared by cucumbers given to you by a man to whom you pay cheese. He swaps the cheese for toilet paper which you use to wrap pasta…and so on. This linking is vital and is another aspect which is missed by most memory techniques. If you can't remember something next in the sequence, you're able to 'skip ahead' to something you *can* remember and then work backwards to the image you'd momentarily forgotten.

This ability to work backwards is what gives the confidence to be able to recall whatever you need to under pressure. This is why I liken this method to scaffolding of a building. You can move around on it, get to the same place from different parts, and the whole things stands secure with each rail, plank, nut and bolt holding the others in place.

We're going to add extra tricks in to make this scaffolding even more secure, but first, let's try another story. Like the planets, this one is going to memorise facts and, also like the planets, I'm not going to tell you what you've just memorised until after you've memorised it! This one is more complicated and longer, so get ready…

Memory Story – The Butler

Picture, if you would, a nicely dressed butler looking very Jeeves and Wooster, carrying dull grey platinum serving plate in one hand. On the plate are some gold goblets and in those are some silver coins, although our Jeeves notices one stray copper coin which he flicks out as a reject. He starts to move and you notice he is gliding – in fact his feet don't even touch the ground! He's lighter than air…

You realise he's going to float away if you're not careful so you tie lead weights to his ankles which help bring him back down. He walks/floats over to a tin-roofed shed and goes inside. Within he sees a man ironing a shirt (perhaps the butlers?) but the man realises he made a mark on the shirt and takes it over to a grey-coloured sink to try and wash it. He scrubs the shirt with what he thinks is a scrubbing brush but it's actually a piece of coal! Now, he's made a real mess and is angry with the coal.

He wraps up the coal in kitchen foil and gets out a light to set fire to it. When he does this it turns out he's lit a fuse which burns distinctly until it reaches the wrapped up silver ball and it then explodes. A chalky white powdery substance falls down like snow and the man rushes to grab a glass to collect some of it. He tastes the stuff he collects – it tastes like salt! Perfect for his dinner. He goes to the stove where there is a pot of something bubbling away and pours the salt into it. Perhaps the butler, who has observed all this, will serve it up on his dish later?

Did you get all that in one go? Well done, if you did – about 20% of my students can remember it flawlessly on the first hearing. The rest get about 90% of it right. If you missed any details, go over it again and test yourself a second time.

If you've done that, you've just memorised one of the key lists needed to be known in most Chemistry courses, and one which causes students plenty of headaches.

The Butler – The Reactivity Series

This is a great memory story because it is so easy to learn (you probably memorised all of it in one reading) and it is also really useful for Chemistry students. The Reactivity Series order the level of reactivity of metals so that you can calculate in reactions which metal will 'kick out' another to form a new compound with something else (usually a non-metal). There are many lists in textbooks and online – some longer than others. I've gone for the one I found most useful to my students over the years which includes hydrogen and carbon in the list. Technically these are not metals (well, carbon isn't and no one is quite sure what to make of Hydrogen which is why it sits alone in most Periodic Tables), but they are often involved in displacement reactions and have their place in terms of reactivity so often get included.

So, how does the story work? The story begins with the least reactive and works up to the most reactive. Where colours are given, these are the colours associated with the elements. Here is the story again, this time with the key words in bold and the element in brackets if it is not directly obvious from the text:

Picture, if you would, a nicely dressed butler looking very Jeeves and Wooster, carrying dull grey platinum serving plate (plate begins with the same letters) in one hand. On the plate are some gold goblets and in those are some silver coins, although our Jeeves notices one stray copper coin which he flicks out as a reject. He starts to move and you notice he is gliding – in fact his feet don't even touch the ground! He's lighter than air (Hydrogen)...

You realise he's going to float away if you're not careful so you tie lead weights to his ankles which help bring him back down. He walks/floats over to a tin-roofed shed and goes inside. Within he sees a man ironing a shirt (perhaps the butler's?) but the man realises he made a mark on the shirt and takes it over to a grey-coloured sink (looks like and rhymes with zinc) to try and wash it. He scrubs the shirt with what he thinks is a scrubbing brush but it's actually a piece of coal (carbon)! Now he's made a real mess and is angry with the coal.

He wraps up the coal in kitchen foil (aluminium) and gets out a lighter to set fire to it. When he does this it turns out he's lit a fuse which burns distinctly (Magnesium which was often used for fuse wires) until it reaches the wrapped up silver ball and it then explodes. A chalky (Calcium well known as chalk – Calcium Carbonate) white powdery substance falls down like snow and the man rushes to grab a glass to collect some of it. He tastes the stuff he collects – it tastes like salt (Sodium well known as a component of salt – Sodium Chloride)! Perfect for his dinner. He goes to the stove where there is a pot (potassium) of something bubbling away and pours the salt into it. Perhaps the butler, who has observed all this, will serve it up on his dish later?

Just to make sure you didn't miss any of the elements, here's the Reactivity Series with the most reactive elements at the top:

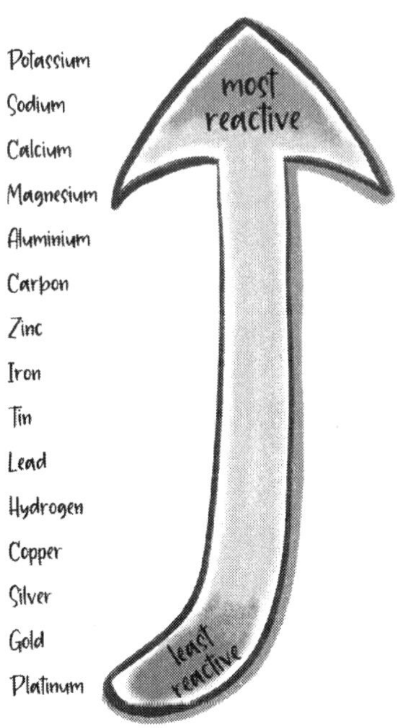

We will return to this particular story later on when we think about taking things further, but for now, this gives you a pretty good idea of the premise. It's really important to notice that in these stories I'm giving you, there's nothing sensible or serious here. Nor are there really any written words or numbers. This is vital. Your images must be as visual as possible. We're really trying to hack into your brain's natural imagination. Indeed, the sillier the stories and images, the better! Make the stories as personal to you as possible to. As we'll see in the consonant system of the next chapter, sometimes the best images you can conjure up are people known to you. Remember these memory stories are personal to you and therefore private. You can have any of these people doing all manner of silly things and need not feel any guilt. In fact, I encourage you to do just that!

There's more to this than just coming up with a silly story however. It's time to add layers and really build up our scaffolding.

Double Entry

One of the (many) courses I've studied and qualified in is bookkeeping. I love keeping track of accounts and working out where money is going. For much of my adult life I've been self-employed and the ability to keep accurate records has been essential. Over the years, I have kept accounts for other small businesses too and I am one of those sad people who really enjoys keeping records. One of the tricks of bookkeeping is something called 'double entry'. This is where you keep both a credit and debit record of accounts and, when totalling everything up, the two entries should come to the same figure. It's a way of making sure that you've not missed something, added up incorrectly, or otherwise made an error in the accounts. As you might imagine, for big businesses doing hundreds of transactions per day, this is an essential technique to make sure records are correct at all times.

We're going to do our own form of 'double entry' wherever possible. As we'll see in the next chapter, sometimes you have several ways to remember the same fact. When that happens, use them! If you have two or more visual images, add them together. This reinforces the memory. Just as you can 'skip ahead' when a memory just won't come to you, sometimes you will remember one particular image better than another.

Memory Palace

Another hack is a very well-known method which has been used for centuries. In fact, Thomas Harris pays homage to this method in his '*Hannibal Lecter*' books about a psychopathic serial killer who has a brilliant mind. As we find out more about Hannibal, we learn he lives in his own memory palace in his mind where all the many things he has memorised are stored.

So what is this palace?

Well, just think about where you live. Regardless of where you are right now, you should be able to picture every room in the house, apartment or halls you live in that's part of your living area. There's a good chance that if you've lived in lots of places, you can picture every room there too. I've lived in so many places that I've forgotten the address and house number of most of them, yet I can see every single room, even with the first house I knew well which I left when I was seven!

We grow strong memories with the places we live then – and not just our dwelling places! There' are our schools, colleges, university departments and places of work. There's our friend's homes and our towns and cities where we live or do a lot of work. So many places we can visualise so well.

Why does this matter? Again, it is about associating – making connections – which our brains love to do so much. By associating the things we want to remember with places we already know, we can mentally 'walk' our way through memories. We did this a little with the shopping list, if you recall? I told you to imagine you were at your local supermarket or shop and to walk into it as a place you know and, crucially, a place associated with food.

When memorising a food list, a food shop is a natural place to set your memory story. Likewise, you can associate rooms in your house (or other buildings or towns etc.) with certain subjects: your kitchen for chemistry, your sitting room for history, your bathroom for biology and so on.

Why do this? Because often the objects we're going to use in our memory stories will reappear for other memories. This is especially true if you need to memorise dates or other numerical data. This means there's a great potential for 'interference' – where one memory clashes with another and you misremember or simply forget both because of the confusion. By associating the memories with certain rooms, you bring clarity to the story and you can keep details separate.

It's not unlike seeing a famous actor in different movies. I don't get the Star Wars and Indiana Jones movies mixed up even though both feature Harrison Ford as a main actor. The settings are completely different and I can make that jump easily. So can most of us, otherwise all actors would feature in one movie only, and then that would be it – career over!

So, if you're memorising several subjects, or modules, or books, at a time – use the memory palace principle and set them apart from one another. You can also do this if you're wanting to separate out centuries when studying history – but we'll come back to the idea when looking at numbers.

Tube map method

A related method to the memory palace is the tube map method. If you've ever looked at the famous London Underground 'Tube' map, you'll see it is a seemingly complex maze of train lines. But look more closely and you can see that most lines are exactly that – lines. Apart from the Circle line which is...er...circular, almost all the others are just bendy lines that crisscross over each other.

This can be useful to us too. When memorising your stories in a memory palace-style room, you will probably be walking around that room as you go from memory to memory. But you can also cut from one side of the room to the other if two separate items actually link up. In effect, what you're doing is creating a 'sub-story' (a bit like a subplot in a movie actually).

For example, I have a student doing A level History who has memorised the dates of the 20th century American Presidents. These all fit into a room set aside for 20th Century events. Each president links on to the next to make a continuous story all the way around the room. But sometimes we want to think about how certain presidents related to, built on policies of, or otherwise contradicted other presidents; and so, they are connected. Or perhaps it is the various 'New Deals' and 'Great Society' programmes of social reform which took place which need to be compared with one another. So, sub-stories need to be made connecting these things, like string from one end of the room to the other cutting through the middle.

An extension for this is simply to have sub-stories trailing off from the main one regardless of whether they link with anything else in the room. So, for instance, perhaps I want to memorise the details of the short few years John F Kennedy was president? While his main story is merely one of taking over from Eisenhower in 1960 to being assassinated in 1963 and Johnson taking over (JFK taking a glass of juice from Eisenhower and turning it into jam which he gives to Johnson – for reasons which will become apparent in the next chapter) – we imagine JFK taking a moment away from the story (juice in hand) to play out a whole separate story which will detail all the various parts of his three years as POTUS. Eventually, he wanders back into line, makes his jam and hands it over to Johnson. Simples. Most of that example will make more sense soon. I promise…

Walk the talk

Remember the poor unfortunate cats mentioned in chapter two? The one who wasn't able to use its legs never learned to 'see' properly. Learning is a physical activity. That's one of the theories why children play with objects so much. They are physically learning about physical things.

Remember too, in chapter three, how I advocated you should do some exercise because it helps stimulate the brain?

Well, we're going to combine these two things now as part of your memory processing. You're going to 'walk the talk' as it were. By that, I mean, as part of your revision process, walk around your room as you go through your memory stories. If you like, or if you can, go to the actual room in the house where you've mentally placed a story and physically walk it as you go from scene to scene.

If that's just not possible, go for a walk outside. As you walk, think through the memory story – or stories – you're practising. Be careful to make sure you're aware of your environment – don't go getting run over crossing a road because you're too busy thinking of butlers carrying plates! – but allow the memories to flow through easily, without too much effort. If one part just isn't coming, stop, concentrate on it, and then move on when you're ready.

There's so many benefits to this part of the system, so don't overlook it. Firstly, exercise is good for you, right? And walking is one of the best things you can do for your body. Then there's the fact that it gets oxygen in your lungs and brings you back to life. Even a five-minute walk after a 20-minute revision session can revitalise your sleepy brain. If nothing else, go walk downstairs to your kitchen for a drink. While you're standing there drinking, revise a memory story. But if you can walk more than that, then this gives you yet another kind of 'double entry'. If you regularly walk a particular place for certain memory stories, then imagining that place when needing to recall can help you bring back those memories sharply.

Talk the talk

While you're walking – assuming you can do this without getting locked up for temporary insanity – talk your memory stories out loud too. Again, this is another way of being active in the memory-forming process. There's plenty of research to suggest this is a good practice in general too. It has been shown that students who listen to recordings of lectures can recall details better than those who just use revision notes. Best of all, however, is students playing back recordings of their *own* notes! If you're someone who really feels the need to write things down, then try this instead. Don't write it – record yourself reading the important information on your phone.

You can play this back while walking if you like, but you can also do it while journeying anywhere by car or train or bus; you can even play it while settling down for sleep in bed at night (please be considerate of others when doing any of this, of course, and wear headphones or similar!). In chapter 8 – Taking it Further, we'll look again at how talking can help.

Practice

Repetitio est mater memoriae. – Repetition is the mother of memory.

Most of these additional tricks have been heading us towards the most important aspect of the system after the actual memory story method itself – how to practise the stories.

As I warned you at the beginning of the book, any mnemonic system which tries to tell you that you'll remember things without any effort is lying (or at least misguided). The very nature of memories is that you need to practise them to reinforce the synaptic links and make them as permanent as possible.

So, how do you practice memory stories? How do you structure your revision timetable? Below is my list of the ways you need to prepare yourself for upcoming exams. I'm going to assume you have at least one year before your exams but you can extend this out for two or more if needed and shorten it if you have an exam which is just a few months away – or less! One of the key aspects of the *Memory Story* method is to make your memories as personal to you as possible. Your method for revising should also be the same. Adapt these suggestions as you see fit, just as you should be with all the tricks and tips given above. If something seems a ghastly idea, you can probably modify it, or drop it if you really have to. Just be careful not to cherry-pick too much. Try to follow these rules as much as possible.

Here's my suggested rules then for ideal preparation for exams:

1) **Don't cram.** Revise every day right from the start. Ideally, by the time you get to an exam there should be no need for 'extra revision' – in fact that is often harmful as new, last-minute information can interfere with other information and leave you confused or misunderstanding. Instead, you want as much memorised securely as possible. Remember how I said that the so-called 'rote learning' so traditionally recommended

works but is inefficient? It works because of the nature of making memories permanent. Refiring those neurons make the synaptic links stronger. The *Memory Story* method hacks into this by using the brain's ability to make connections with other memories and finds a short cut to recall. But you still have to make those memories permanent. Rather than hours spent writing out, or reciting, endless lists of facts to learn, your memory stories should take minutes.

2) **20-minute learning.** I absolutely definitely, beyond a doubt *don't want you studying longer than 20 minutes at a time.* This might sound like crazy talk, I know, but it's true. This doesn't mean you just study for 20 minutes and then pack up for the day. I mean, you need to break your study periods into smaller chunks and break them up with different activities.

   One of the many subjects I teach is music and that includes teaching piano, guitar and saxophone. With my musician hat on, I used to help students find time to practise their instruments by pointing out that they will study and do homework better if they take regular breaks and practise their instrument for a short time in between. Their mind stays active, yet they give their brain a break from the hard slog of studying.

   You don't need to take up an instrument (though if you already play an instrument then absolutely use it to break up your study), but do take active breaks. This is the time to go for a walk to practise your memory stories. Or take the water break and go to the kitchen. Stand up and 'walk the talk', or even just change where you're sitting and choose a different topic area to study. Anything you can do which keeps your mind active and breaks up the study period into small time chunks which keep your mind fresh. Which leads nicely to the next rule...

3) **No screen time.** Absolutely avoid watching TV, playing on your phone, or any other thing which is distracting and allows your mind to go into stand-by mode. Not only do you risk taking

a much longer break than you intended (when I go on to my phone for 'five minutes' I inevitably lose about 30 minutes – I blame alien abduction to be honest…), but you make it much harder for your brain to 'restart' once it has started to turn off.

There are evolutionary reasons for this. It's why we feel sleepy after a big meal. When we eat, it should be because we're hungry. When we're hungry, it means the body is running out of energy and needs to replenish stocks. It takes time though for digestion to break down the food we eat and absorb it into our bloodstream to get all the nutrients to our cells. So the body goes into sleep mode to use the minimum of energy while we 'stock up'. For our ancestors, sleeping during the day was generally a bad idea with predators around (though in very hot countries the 'siesta' became a thing because even the predators find shade and go to sleep during that time!), and so we gradually fell to eating at night (when we can do very little in the dark anyway) and sleeping afterwards.

When you take a non-active break then, your body thinks it is time to wind down and call it a day, because we're genetically wired to associate 'not doing' with conserving energy. So don't do it. Make your breaks active, but just *different* to the study you were doing.

4) **Avoid writing notes.** Below I will talk about this and provide you with sheets to copy and use for your memory stories themselves, if you're the kind of person who feels they must *write something*. But that's about the limit of it. You won't have those sheets in the exam and the idea of 'writing notes' is a throwback to the idea of rote learning. It's fine to make notes in lessons, lectures, from library books etc., where you feel you need details to use in an essay or to aid understanding. But once you've fully grasped a concept or topic, start committing it to memory NOW. The only notes you should make, apart from drawing or listing out your stories if you really

need to, is to make a list of the things you've memorised so that you can make a rota for practising them. Which leads nicely on to the next rule!

5) **1:1:1 method.** This is a super idea I picked up about ten years ago and I've used ever since. To explain it, let me remind you of the theories of memory and the physiology of memory again.

Remember, a memory is a very real, tangible, physical piece of hardware. Your neurons really are making connections with each other with those twiglike dendrites and axons. But your brain is doing that all the time and immediately breaking down most connections. It is only repetition which makes the connections remain. Over time, some connections, if not used, will begin breaking down again. Others, which are well-practised, don't break down at all.

Practically, what this means is that new memories need to be refreshed sooner, longer-term memories need refreshing from time to time. Only permanent memories don't need refreshing at all – although I say that with caution as there is evidence to show that there really isn't any such thing as a permanent memory. For instance, many people who learn a new language and immerse themselves in the culture of the language for a long time, claim that they start to forget words in their home language as they become more fluent and natural in the new. Part of this is interference – the new language you're using all the time, 'dominates' and makes it hard to remember the original words you knew – but some of it is simply disuse of your home language that, after many years, begins to break down.

The 1:1:1 method adapts your revision to the way your brain works. When you come home from your lessons (or finish your study period) immediately set to work making your new learning into a memory story. Then test that story ***one hour*** later. After that, revise it again ***one day*** later. If all is secure, set it in your diary to revise ***one week*** later. If that is still secure, then revise it *at least* every month, though for shorter courses you might want to keep it booked in for once a week.

The 'one hour then one day' part reinforces in the mind that this is a memory that is going to be needed. If you find that the memory story begins to be a bit fragile at the 'once a week' stage, then go back to learning it afresh, practise an hour later, practise the next day and so on until it is secure enough to go back to once a week. Once you have it established as a 'medium term' memory, then the task is to keep it refreshed at manageable regular intervals so the synaptic links aren't allowed to break down. Indeed, after a few months of this, those memories are going to start to feel permanent. That's a dangerous time, because they're *not*. Make sure you read Chapter 8 – *'Taking it Further'* – to see how to avoid the mistake of thinking you can ditch memory stories when everything is well learned.

Keeping notes – TNTL sheets

The beauty of the TNTL *Memory Story* method is that there is no real reason to ever make notes again. Why would you need to? You're spending the bulk of your revision time working on the memory stories themselves using your imagination. After all, you won't have your notes in your exams.

But I appreciate that, in the early days at least, you might feel the need to write down the basic gist of the stories, or the details of what you're memorising. Or perhaps you'd prefer to draw your memory stories? After all, they are images you're seeing. So why not draw them?

For just that kind of person, I am including a template sheet you can use for yourself. You'll find lots of copies in the back but here's one for you to look at now:

It should be self-explanatory how to use this, but just to make sure, here’s what the Planet’s memory story might look like:

I know, I know – I'm a pretty amazing artist, right? Yeah…not so much. I'm pretty awful at drawing, to be honest, which is why I never try. These pictures – like all the images in this book – are the creation of my super-talented illustrator.

In the next chapter we'll look at one of the trickiest things any student has to deal with: numbers.

EXERCISE:

Revise the memory stories you've learnt so far – even if you have no need of any scientific memorising – to practise reinforcing memories and get used to memorising in this way. Although we still have many principles to go yet, you can start trying to memorise information you actually need for yourself at the same time. Remember, there's no limit to how many stories you can hold in your head but do assign places to each one using the Memory Palace principle.

Chapter 5 – Memorising numbers

I'm going to kick off with another story right away this time…

Memory Story – Seeing Red

Imagine you're holding a lump of coal which is making you so excited to hold that your heart is thumping hard. The coal has been fashioned into something – a doorknob! But it is still a piece of coal so you're able to draw a black line on the ground with this knob. You get bored of this and throw it into a huge round fire that's near you. As soon as you do so, the fire spits out flames which set fire to the rug in front. You rush to find something to put out the flames and notice a jar of water which you use. Smoke rises but you realise it is filling a balloon in the sky with lots of air. The balloon is attached to a gate and you see a man starting to undo the string holding it. He is wading through mucky fertilizer soil which is difficult because he's really fat and is sinking into the muck like it was quicksand. He pulls himself out but without shoes for which he has to push his hands into the soil to retrieve them! Finally, he cleans his hands in a nice bowl of bubbling fiery liquid which is behind its own gate and he stirs the liquid with a metal bar, then pours the liquid over a door.

We're going to kick off with perhaps the most daunting and difficult memory work that any student has to cope with: numbers! Trying to remember dates, figures, telephone numbers, chemical formula and more is, without help, very difficult (and for some of us, completely impossible). Fear not! You need to learn just two systems and numbers will no longer cause you any problem at all.

Remember though that you will need to practise and work at this to become a system you're fluent with and can use at a drop of a hat. You'll find with the following that you'll be able to memorise birthdays and telephone numbers too, so even beyond the world of academic study, it's a really useful tool.

The Peg Number System

This technique simply associates objects that sound like the numbers with the numbers themselves. Here's my personal list but by the side I've put a few alternatives. You might think of even better objects – feel free to use your own ones. In fact, it is better if you do because they will mean more to you and so you'll remember them better.

KEY POINT TO REMEMBER – always go for objects and people that seem most natural for you. These are the things that come to your mind first each time. You want your memory aids to be no effort to remember or you will struggle.

Here's the list then:

One – bun; pond; wand; scone

Two – shoe; food; loo (slang for toilet); poo (yuck!)

Three – tree; knee; wii (the game console); wee (yuck again!)

Four – door; chore; floor

Five – hive; tribe; knife

Six – sticks; tricks; pricks; wicks

Seven – heaven; leaven(ed bread); Devon (place in the UK particularly known for its cream teas!); Kevin (if you know someone called Kevin)

Eight – gate; mate; crate

Nine – wine; mine; shine

Ten – hen; pen; men

I use this list all the time. Personally, the objects I use are the ones which are first in each line (bun, shoe, tree, door etc.). Choose your favourites and stick to them. This is such a simple system to use and you can get on with using it straight away. It is particularly useful if you need to memorise a list that needs doing in order or if you have, say, five things about Julius Caesar you need to recall in an exam. You simply attach your memory for the first thing to a bun and your second fact to a shoe and so on. You can now put these objects into your 'memory rooms' where you need to make lists of facts to remember. You're going to have buns and shoes flying around all over the place when you start doing lots of memorising but they won't interfere with each other as long as you attach these things to different 'rooms'.

The Consonant System

Now, the problem comes when you have longer numbers to remember. You could memorise a 10-digit phone number using the peg system but then you have ten objects to try and keep in order. What if we could make it half that amount? We can – but it needs a more sophisticated system: *The Consonant system.*

Again, this idea has been around a long time – centuries for certain, as Stanislaus Mink von Wennsshein apparently first started formulating it in the 1600s. It was developed in the next century by Richard Grey, although he made it rather complicated in doing so. Traditionally, it is known as the *'Major System'* but no one really seems to know why. So, here I give you my personal take on it and I call it a much more sensible name as you will, no doubt, agree present!y!

This time, instead of associating objects with the numbers, we're going to attach consonants. No vowels – you'll see why – just consonant letters. Here's the list of numbers along with their corresponding letters and the reasoning for why we're using those letters:

0 – Z, S – Z for Zero. Z and S sound similar to each other.

1 – T, D – 't' uses just ONE main stroke. 't' and 'd' sound similar to each other.

2 – N – if you turn 2 on its side it looks like an 'n'.

3 – M – Again, turn 3 on its side and it looks like an 'm'.

4 – R – Trickier this one. If you spell out FOUR the last letter is an 'r'.

5 – L – This is the hardest. It looks like an 'S' but we've used that for zero. 50 in Roman numerals is L – if you don't know your Roman numerals, you should. They still get used a lot – especially in book prefaces.

6 – G, J – a lowercase 'g' looks like 6 reversed and turned upside down. A soft 'g' sound sounds like 'j' so both letters are possible even though you can also make the 'g' into a hard sound too. So we will be able to remember 'Game' or 'jab' and both remind us of the number 6 (Game is 63, jab is 69).

7 – K – if you look carefully at the letter K you'll see it is made up of lots of '7's put together!

8 – F or V – When handwriting an f the swirl looks like an incomplete 8. The sound of an 'f' (that 'fuh' sound') is similar to the sound of 'v' ('vuh'). So both letters are associated with 8.

9 – P or B – the number looks like a P which has been reversed. It also looks like an upside-down lowercase 'b' (which also has a similar sound to 'p' too).

That's it! You need to memorise this list but the good news is most of it is really obvious and easy to remember (5 as L is the hardest to get used to if you don't know Roman numbers). And you can learn as you practice.

So how do we use these? Basically, you memorise pairs of numbers by putting the consonants together and 'filling in' with vowels to make and object (or, if necessary, an action). It can be anything as long as you can really see it clearly. You also work phonetically rather than spelling things correctly. It's how the word *sounds* that matters. The following examples will help you to understand.

Examples:

13 = t or d (for 1) and m (for 3)

Possible words:

Tim (if you know someone by this name or a famous person comes to mind)

Dam (like a beaver's dam or reservoir dam)

Time (like a clock face or watch)

49 = 4 (for 4) and p or b (for 9)

Possible words:

Rope

Rob (like robbing a bank or a person called Rob if you know someone)

Rape

Rap

Rib

Rip (like ripping something open)

57 = L (for 5) and K (for 7)

Possible words:

Lucky (perhaps an image of someone winning at Roulette)

Lock

Lick (someone licking something else)

26 = n (for 2) and j or g (for 6)

Possible words:

Nudge (someone nudging someone or something else)

Nag (an old horse or someone 'nagging' someone else)

82 = f or v (for 8) and n (for 2)

Possible words:

Fan

Van

Phone (phonetically still 'f' and 'n' sounds)

Fin

Fun

You see how it works? I could give you a complete list of numbers from 11 to 99 (for single figures use the Peg system) but the best way to use the Consonant System is to come up with words for yourself. The more relatable the objects are to yourself, the better. Ideally, when first coming up with an object for a number, go for the first object which really grabs you. For instance, with 82 for me it's the fan which sticks in my head – so I use that.

People you know are also really useful that way. In my last school where I was teaching this memory method to students there was a teacher known to all students as 'Deb'. She was the first name we thought of whenever wanting to memorise the number 19 and even now, many years later, I still use her as my 'object' for that number. I could use 'tip', 'tap', 'top', or 'tub' just as easily – but I prefer to think of Deb. Her mannerisms and character shine out and that makes her great to remember! So if the names of friends, family, teachers, or even famous people, come to mind when you're searching for words to fit your numbers, go ahead and use them! I use people I know literally many dozens of times with my memory stories.

The key thing to remember is that whatever you come up with, make sure it is really *visual.* That means, for most of the time, coming up with objects. Sometimes, you might use verbs, but be careful to make sure you can really 'see' the action if so. For instance, for 82 above I said 'fun' could be used. But what is 'fun'? How do you show someone having 'fun' without confusing it for other actions like laughing or dancing and so on? I'd stick to an object like 'van', if I have the option. 24, however, I use 'gnaw'. This is something quite unmistakable. Having someone, or something, 'gnawing' away at something else is really visual. It's my go-to image for 24.

If you work at all the memory stories in this book (including those in the appendix) you'll get plenty of practise at all the words I like to use for numbers from 1 to 64 at the very least, and a good number of the rest until 99. But really, it is more important for you to try and form your own. The act of working hard to come up with a decent object or action to make your memory is another way of making your brain concentrate on the memory at hand and help it make good strong synaptic links.

And don't forget the 'double entry' trick I taught you in the last chapter! As you've seen from the above examples, you often have two or more objects which could be used. So use them. For 82 then, I could imagine someone in a 'van' holding a 'fan' in one hand and a 'fin' in the other. That's three images to give me 82.

One final thing before I go on to 'reveal' the *'Seeing Red'* story. Do you remember the principle of the *Memory Palace* in chapter four? Well, this works wonderfully well with the Consonant System when it comes memorising historical dates. You split the dates into two separate two-digit numbers. The first pair - the century - you assign a room to and associate everything in it with the appropriate object. So you have a 1500s room with a doll being passed from scene to scene; a 1800s room with a dove flying around.

This is so helpful I actually get my students to remember dates even when they don't need to because the dates are so simple to memorise that you can attach more complex ideas to them and recall difficult information far more reliably. For instance, most people acknowledge that Quantum Physics is one of the most complicated subjects to keep track of while you're learning the principles. Inevitably, textbooks go back in history to chart the progress of research in order to teach the fundamentals. So you'll get Young in 1801, Hertz in 1885, Becquerel in 1896, Rutherford in 1899-1903, then Planck, Einstein, Hess, Bohr, Heisenberg, Fermi, Dirac...and many, many more. It is quite intimidating – but the memory palace, using the consonant system to create memory stories, will handle them all.

Seeing Red – Haemoglobin

The "Seeing Red" memory story is useful because it shows how we can combine number methods together and use prior knowledge to help build images. You've just learned an incredibly complicated chemical formula for haemoglobin – the part of your blood that makes it red.

Here's the formula:

$\mathbf{C_{2952}H_{4664}O_{832}N_{812}S_{8}Fe_{4}}$

As you can see, it's a humdinger, isn't it? Normally this would be a difficult piece of information to remember (and indeed it is not required in any chemistry or biology course I know of, probably because it *is* so bonkers), which is perfect for us to see how simple things become when you give them a story.

The numbers are split mostly into 2-digit codes with the occasional 1-digit one thrown in. The important aspect here is that we've added the chemicals into the mix. Carbon (C) is the coal. Hydrogen (H) is basically what the Sun is composed of (it's a huge hydrogen reactor, effectively) so I picture it as a 'round fire'. Oxygen (O) we know best as the component of air we all breathe and so I pictured a balloon filling with air. Nitrogen is a key component of fertilizer (as most Chemistry students should know) so I used that image. Sulphur (S) in Biblical imagery makes up the 'fiery lakes of Hell' so I used that graphic image. Finally, Iron (Fe) is fairly obvious – anything metal should do the job.

Note that the images I've given are the ones easiest for me and make use of the prior knowledge I've already gained. There's no point imagining fertilizer if you don't know that nitrogen is a key part. This is why I said at the beginning that memory aids only help if you've understood the subject matter you're studying first. Indeed, I'm also assuming you know that these letters stand for chemicals and you know that *Fe* is the recognised symbol for Iron, and so on.

Putting it together, we start with our excited hearts (reminding us we're doing blood here) as we hold coal (Carbon) in the shape of a knob (29) and then draw a line (52). Then we move on to fire (Hydrogen) which sets a rug (46) aflame until put out by water from a jar (64) and so on. Note that Oxygen's 832 I split into 8 and 32 but Nitrogen's 812 I split into 81 and 2 rather than 8 and 12 simply to avoid too many 8s appearing (there's two in my story instead of three).

And that's it - numbers made simple! When I first start teaching this system, I often get my students to memorise Pi to twenty decimal places. You'll find that story in the appendix if you fancy doing that one, except that I've extended it beyond the ten memory images you need for twenty decimal places. Why not have a go and see how easy it is and how many decimal places you can get to? It takes literally two minutes of telling the story for my students to have Pi done to twenty decimal places. It's far too easy really!

EXERCISE:

Practise the 'Seeing Red' story until you're confident of writing out the formula correctly. While you're at it, try memorising your phone number, other phone numbers, your bank account details, and/or all the birthdays for your family and friends. With birthdays you'll need two numbers – one for the month, and one for the day. When you've done some of these, try developing your work into longer lists. Take a look at the appendix for stories which will really test your use of the consonant system.

Chapter 6 – Memorising languages

You would think that words are easy to remember compared to numbers but, as we've seen, numbers are easy once you have a good system such as the Consonant or Peg system. Words are trickier, partly because we're so familiar with using them that we don't pay words the attention they need. When it comes to learning a foreign language, the task can often feel too much of an uphill struggle because we don't have any method for dealing with new, unfamiliar words. This is made even worse if the new language has a completely new script attached to it!

I'm going to describe how to learn the alphabets and characters for non-Latin-based languages first, and then deal with memorising words for all languages. It may seem strange to put scripts first (most people recoil in horror at the thought of learning Bengali, Korean or, worse of all, Chinese) but, as we shall see, this isn't true when we apply the underlying principle of the best memory methods: Visualising!

I will also say I'm assuming that as you're happy reading this book in English that you consider English at least a 'home' language even if it isn't necessarily your birth language.

Learning foreign language scripts

There are so many different language scripts around the world today. There's at least 20 major scripts in use (such as the Latin one used for English and European languages and the Arabic used throughout the Middle East), but with something in the region of nearly 4,000 languages recorded as having an established writing system, the reality is that there are many divisions and subdivisions of these scripts.

I am not, therefore, going to spoon-feed you how to memorise every letter of all (or even any) scripts. What I will do is show you examples from several languages so that you get the idea and can start to use it on whatever language or languages you're studying. Even if you're not studying a language at the moment, don't skip this part: it teaches valuable principles. Besides which, you never know when it would be helpful to pick up a language or two!

Bengali	ক	ko		K
Bengali	ব	bo		b
Arabic	ل	laam		L
Korean	ㅃ	pp	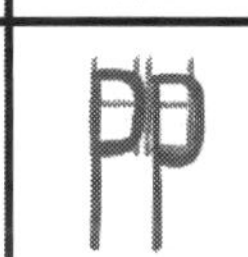	pp

The table above shows you the principles I outline below. The main trick to non-Latin-based scripts is to turn letters into pictures you can see which will give you the sound you need to remember or, in the case of Chinese, the word you need to remember as well. Sometimes that could actually be an English letter. Take Bengali, for instance. Several letters of the Bengali script can be seen to look like English ones.

'Ka' or 'Ko' (a 'K' sound in Bengali) looks like a K put on its side.

'Ba' or 'Bo' is a partial 'b' which is reversed.

The same with other language scripts:

Arabic – The Arabic 'laam' is an 'L' sound and looks just like one which has been reversed.

Korean -The Korean lettering for a 'pp' sound looks partially like the 'pp' lettering itself.

I could go on, but you get the idea I think. This won't work with all letters but where you can see the English equivalent hidden inside, use that.

The next stage, for more difficult letters, is to use anything which will give you an image. Let's take the Korean for 'K'. Look up the Korean alphabet online and have a look at the letter which sounds like K.

Unfortunately, if anything, this letter looks more like a back-to-front 'F'. But we can use that. It looks like F, which is the first letter of 'FORK' which the symbol also looks a little like. Imagine using a primitive fork like that and trying to eat with it! Now, if you're studying Korean you'll quickly realise that there is no sound for an 'F' at all – so we know this symbol can't mean 'F'. But in the word 'FORK' there is an K at the end. It's the K which we want.

So, when you see this letter, you immediately visualise eating with a simple fork that looks like the letter and exaggerate saying 'forKKKKK' to yourself. It won't take many repetitions for this image and the correct sound of 'K' to stick in your head.

Strangely enough, one of the hardest languages to learn is also one of the easiest to memorise: Chinese. Pronunciation is a different issue, but in terms of reading the characters, it's a breeze because, unlike most other languages, the characters already represent pictures. Although it can be argued that long ago our English letters had pictorial references, they've long since lost any sense of being pictures. Chinese characters haven't. Even if you don't know what each segment of a character is supposed to mean, you can make images out of it to help you memorise. With a little thought though, you can 'add' to the pictures to give you the sounds of the Chinese too. Here's some examples to get you started:

Chinese

山	shān		Mountain (shone)
出	chū		Exit (chute)
古	gǔ		Ancient (goo)
叶	yè		Leaf (yeah)

Look carefully at this table. The first column lists four common Chinese characters. The second lists the pronunciation. The symbols over the letters refer to which 'tone' to use which isn't of importance to us here but would be important if you're going to learn the language comprehensively. The third column shows my visualisations of the characters into the objects they represent. Chinese is really easy for this. 'Mountain' already really looks like one. 'Ancient' you can easily imagine as an 'ancient' gravestone. 'Leaf' doesn't take much imagination to see that leaves flitter around in the wind and the wind is so strong it has knocked the 'ancient' gravestone over!

But then I've added extra details. The sun rising over the mountains means it 'shone' – which sounds close enough to the Chinese pronunciation 'shan'. 'Exit' is via a 'chute' slipping between two mountains – 'chu'. Horrid body 'goo' is leaking out of the grave – 'gu'.

And a Mary Poppins-like character is enjoying the wind with her legendary umbrella and going 'yeah!' as she flies – 'ye'.

More complex Chinese words build up by using these simpler characters, adapting them slightly in some cases. This is great – they give you their very own memory story! For instance, the character for 'compile/edit' uses the characters for 'car', 'mouth' and 'ear'. You could imagine someone driving around in a car picking up body parts of mouths and ears to 'compile' them together in some kind of government account! Look it up and see how that looks.

In fact, if you're really interested in learning Chinese, I *hugely* recommend a superb book by Alan Hoenig called *'Chinese Characters: Learn and remember 2178 characters and their meanings'*. It does exactly what it says on the tin. He uses the same principle of making visual stories although he doesn't go as far as I do in providing ways to remember the sounds. Nevertheless, the book gives you the majority of characters you'd ever use and useful ideas for each one to remember them. Follow my examples here and you'll add the sounds into your stories with ease.

Memorising words

Again, there's no point trying to go through lots of words in lots of languages – there's just too many out there. All I will do then, is give you a few examples of the kind of work you have to do for yourself.

If you're dealing with a language which is closely related to ours – basically, most European languages fit into this category, like French, Italian, German and Spanish – then the first step is to find out as many words as you can which are identical, or almost identical to ours. Often, the similarity is actually because the English pinched the word from another language! English is the magpie of the language world, stealing 'shiny' words all the time. Even languages you might think are fairly unconnected – like Hindi – have lots of words which are the same. 'Shampoo' is one which comes to mind (and again, the English stole it from the Indians – we have no shame…)

You'll be surprised just how many words don't need memorising at all. While English has taken many of its common words from other cultures, it has also become the 'lingua franca' of the world and that means many languages borrow back from the English. While I was learning Bengali, during my years in Bangladesh, I discovered that there are Bengali words for: television, chair, bottle, Biology and Physics. I also discovered almost no Bangladeshi actually uses those words or, often, even know that those words exist at all! They just use the English. I used to find it bizarre. "It's your language," I'd say to my students, "use it!" But over the years I've come to think 'whatever' instead because, frankly, we're all mixing and matching with our home languages today.

That said, there's still far more words which sound completely different than sound the same, so we have to deal with these. To memorise these, we need to make sound connections with words we do know. Usually, these will be from our home language; but if you already speak more than one language, you may find connections can be made with words from somewhere else instead.

I am randomly choosing a language which is pretty largely unconnected with English – Korean. I'm not going to write them in script here. I'll use the phonetic pronunciation instead and take you through how I would memorise these words. This way, you'll see how, even with a language very different to our own, you can create memory stories nevertheless.

Notice how I don't need to get pronunciations exactly right. Just as with our main studying for academic subjects, I expect you to be learning and understanding the material before memorising. With languages, that means listening to pronunciation and practising saying the words correctly. From there, you just need a memory story to 'jog' the recall where you'll say the words accurately.

Good morning/hello/good evening/bye – an-nyeong-ha-se-yo

I picture someone I know called 'Ann' holding a 'neon' light in her hand, waving at us, laughing, saying 'ha' and rapping going 'say yo!'. She does this as the sun rises, during the day, and as the sun sets too and even as she waves goodbye! (Ann-neon-ha-say-yo)

Goodbye – jal-ga / tto man-na-yo

Another way to say goodbye, Ann is too busy playing with a toy tiger to do anything other than wave bye. (ti-ger sounds like jal-ga). But she drops the tiger on her foot and it turns out to be really heavy! She cries out "Toe! My nail!" (tow-mah-nay-ul)

Maybe – a-ma-do

Asking a sulky child if they are going to do something or not, they say to you, with a heavy dialect, "I might do." (Ah mah doh)

Thank you – gam-sa-ham-ni-da

Before saying thank you to a boy called Sam, you need to tell him to come over to help because you need him – "Come Sam, I need yer!" (Kam-Sam-need-ya)

Hopefully, you get the idea from all this and – assuming you are studying a language – you can start applying this principle to the vocabulary lists you have to learn for any language course.

EXERCISE:

Even if you are not formally studying a language, or have no intention of brushing up on your French before you go on holiday to Paris soon, it is worth taking the time to learn a few words of a language to practise the principle. Choose one you might be interested in, look up the most used 30, 50, 100 or 500 words in the language (depending on just how much you want to try) and get stuck in!

Just like the fuller *Memory Story* method, you can string whole collections of words together into one story if you wish. So, you could memorise a list of body parts, or vegetables, or days of the week, and so on, into one longer story.

Just to egg you on - if you're thinking languages aren't for you - I'll tell you I can already read, write and speak Bengali, have a smattering of Hindi and can get along in an obscure language called 'Santali', spoken in the North Bengal region. I know quite a bit of French and am semi-reasonable at Latin and Greek. I am studying Chinese (I teach a lot of Chinese students English online, so it's helpful and, frankly, only fair) and – wait for this – Ancient Egyptian Hieroglyphics. I jest not. I actually have a qualification in Hieroglyphs.

Yet, I was rubbish at languages at school and I would say I'm pretty poor at speaking them. My students in Bangladesh used to giggle at me when speaking Bengali. They understood what I said (and apparently my Bengali handwriting is superb), but I always sound like an Englishman speaking Bengali. Oh well, you can't have everything…The point is, I'm no natural language learner, and yet I can pick up any language I like using these techniques. So can you.

Chapter 7 – Memorising People

Time for painfully honest admission: I'm appalling at remembering faces.

This is such an embarrassing thing to admit. Being a classroom teacher for fifteen years, I got to see what felt like vast seas of faces on a daily basis. There was something of an expectation among teachers that you would always remember your students. There were various tricks taught in teacher training college of how to help you remember them all quickly – like make seating plans so your students sit in the same seat for each class with you. Oddly, those teaching that technique didn't realise this worked because of the *memory palace* idea – associating a memory with a specific place – but it worked nonetheless.

The downside was that even when their names and faces were fixed in my mind in the classroom, if I saw students in the street, I would struggle to realise it unless I knew them well. To this day, when I see a student, or former student, in the street, there's a good chance I will not be sure if I know them or not. Luckily, I'm a nice guy and I tend to smile sweetly at anyone who seems to show some recognition of me. So, generally, no one is any the wiser when I raise a smile and a hand in a wave. They have no idea I'm thinking "who the heck are you?!"

There are times, however, when it is essential to remember names and faces: your new boss, a new colleague, the girl/boy who's just joined your class and you have a definite crush on, your new girl or boyfriend (Disclaimer: yes, I've forgotten the name of people I was dating in the past. Really. My memory is *that* bad).

When I've needed to remember who someone is, I've applied memory stories to them. It's not an easy task for me, but it does work if I'm prepared to put in the effort. There's certainly no better way - except by repetition and the embarrassment of saying, every time I meet them, "I'm so sorry, but could you tell me your name again?"

How do we memorise people then? Well, here's an exercise to get you started. I didn't want to use faces of real people with real names for a whole host of reasons (not least the expense of legalities) but mostly because I couldn't trust myself to be unbiased in choosing names and faces I might just find easy. So, I had my long-suffering illustrator come up with a load of faces with as minimal conditions set as possible – just that they must come from a variety of backgrounds and ages. I then put up these caricatures onto social media and asked followers to come up with names for these six characters. I then chose the best names from the list compiled. The result is a semi-random selection of characters and names to work on.

Another reason for having caricatures drawn is that facial features are slightly exaggerated. This is helpful in training because it is the most important facial features of a person you are going to use to form your memory stories. When you've got used to the technique here, try it with photos of people on the internet. Then, when you're ready, move on to use it in life with real people.

Before going on to the technique itself, I'd like to share one more personal story which highlights the importance of knowing who a person is. It is, in many ways, the nicest thing you could do for a stranger.

When I was a classroom teacher, I had a form group of around thirty kids who I looked after for five years at a time. They would start at my school aged eleven and they were really still very much little junior school children; I would have the privilege of seeing them growing up into young adults by the time they left school at sixteen. When one cohort left, I was assigned a new group of 11-year-olds to start the tutoring again. These kids I saw every single morning to register them and give them updates they needed to know. I also taught them for various classes.

One cohort, before they moved into the school, I was given a set of cards – one for each student – with a photo of their face and details of who they were, their date of birth and their previous junior school. I was very aware that these poor little lads and lasses were often moving from schools of only dozens of children, which they'd known their whole short lives, and into my school which was huge and had over 1500 students, *all* of whom were older and bigger. It must have been very scary for them, even though it was also exciting.

So, I spent the evening before I met them memorising every single detail about them. Bear in mind what I said earlier about how bad I am at remembering faces – yet it took me no more than about an hour to memorise 30 faces and then another half hour perhaps to revise them later in the evening. I revised them again in the morning before going to work.

When I met my new form group, I was instantly asking students by name to do this or do that. I chatted to them using their names too. When doing the register, I was able to link up which two or three students had come from such-a-such school and was also able to comment on when their birthdays were – all from memory.

The students went home raving to their parents about how welcome they had felt, that their very first teacher already knew who they were and knew all about them. To know someone as a person is a precious gift to give them. My form group felt safe in a scary new environment and we bonded tightly from day one. At the time of writing, I left them for pastures new twelve years ago, yet most of them still stay in some form of contact with me – through Facebook, or Instagram etc – and when I see them in town they are always pleased to see me. I'm proud of them – they've all grown into great men and women – but I'm also proud of myself for taking the effort to do that one simple thing which meant so much at the time.

Learn the names of those you meet. It's a gift to use a name.

Memory technique for faces and names

Below are the caricatures of six characters from various backgrounds. Have a good look at them now.

The first stage when memorising faces is to focus on the faces as much as possible to identify what stands out. If you're chatting to someone for the first time, this is actually a social good thing to do. It will look like you're making proper eye contact with them and engaging in who they are – and we all like it when someone pays us attention! However, be careful not to stare at them and spend too long looking at some part of their head – good attention swiftly looks like creepiness!

If you're dealing with a photo, then there's no worrying about creepiness (thankfully!) but most of the time you'll be dealing with new people in the real world. Either way, take time to really notice the key detail or details about the person. Hoshi Ito is a big smiler and has 'oriental' looks about him. Freddie has a pointed, bearded chin. Oscar is balding and has sad eyebrows. Anita has sharp, angular eyebrows and nose. Sharon has a big mouth and very frizzy hair. Hilary has a big forehead and thin straight eyebrows. Just as these caricatures have already done a little, in your mind, you really want to exaggerate these features now so you can see each person with comically altered faces and heads to make the features prominent.

Secondly, if talking with someone, you can quickly pick up something of their character. This is important. A sense of what kind of person they are helps to remember them. From pictures we're going to have to do this from the impression we get from the images (if you then meet the person in real life, you might have to adjust your impression as pictures can often be deceiving). I find Hoshi to be someone who loves life and loves laughing. Freddie is a bit of a 'cool' guy. Oscar is an older man who looks like he enjoys the simple life. Anita looks serious and intelligent – she doesn't suffer fools gladly! Sharon looks like a bit of a mischievous joker. Hilary looks like a very well-to-do older woman who expects the fine things in life.

The third stage can be worked on after you have met the person – rather than while you're chatting to them – but do it straightaway. You need to find objects or actions which you can associate with their name. Start by saying their name over and over again – this is our equivalent of 'learning the subject'. As usual, we might come up with things which loosely sound like the actual name, so this repetition of their name is important – otherwise you might end up calling them all sorts of strange things when you meet them again!

Hoshi Ito – Horsey, eat toes.

Freddie Treadgold – My grandfather was a Freddie, so I can think of him, or I can think of a chocolate bar called 'Freddos' that is well-loved here. Treading on gold is obvious.

Oscar Farnway – The Oscars are famous film trophies which are instantly recognisable. Farm way.

Anita Rupal – A neat(er) person. Rupees – gold coins from India. Or I could use 'rope' as close enough.

Sharon Mensah – I've known a few Sharon's so I could use one of them, or 'cha run' – running with cups of cha (tea). Men's…??

Hliary Osbourne – I know the face and name of America's Hilary Clinton very well and Osbourne makes me think of rock star Ozzy Osbourne. Alternatively, 'hilarious' and Wizard of Oz being born (Oz born).

Last stage – put it all together. This is the time to create a memory story linking all the parts together. If the name is the same as someone you know, add them to the picture. Where you have a couple of options, put both in, as per the 'double entry' technique.

Here's my memory stories then:

Hoshi Ito – *He's riding a horse and smiling hugely while pulling his foot up to eat his toes.*

Freddie Treadgold – *He's such a cool guy that he's dancing around and starts walking on his chin, which is so pointy it is picking up gold pieces on the floor while he treads on them. At the same time, my grandfather, Freddie, is handing him Freddos to eat upside down.*

Oscar Farnway – *He's actually walking on a large version of his own head! The forehead is a big field with the hair on either side bushes and trees. That's because he's walking the way to his Farm. All the while he's happy as he walks because he's won an Oscar for a film role which he's clutching in his hands.*

Anita Rupal – *She is immaculately dressed and tidying the perfect house to make it even neater while finding many Indian rupees down the side of sofas, to put into her vastly overflowing money box. This is a wealthy lady! Everything in the house is as sharp and angular as* *her facial features. She won't be happy if you mess up her room – she's looking at you sternly right now!*

Sharon Mensah – *She's watching a Men's Cha Run. She's at the front of the crowd as the men race by with cups of tea in their hands. Very naughtily, she's thinking of sticking her foot out to trip one of them over, and she's nervously playing with her springy hair which is going 'boing' every time she lets go!*

Hilary Osbourne – *Hilary Clinton and Ozzy Osbourne are sitting with this lady having very dignified chats, If you know Ozzy Osbourne then this image is hilarious. Indeed, they all find something hilarious and laugh raucously. Meanwhile, our lady is holding a newborn baby – who is dressed like the Wizard of Oz!*

Despite my personal story of my form group and this exercise you've just read through, you won't often have to memorise a lot of names and faces in one go. But hopefully, you've just seen how easy it is to do six. Learning one at a time will be easier still. Nevertheless, you might find it takes you a few meetings with a person before the memory sticks. That's fine – people aren't usually offended on the second meeting anyway if you've forgotten the name. Just re-revise the memory story and it will come together more the second time around.

You might feel I cheated with names like 'Treadgold' and 'Rupal' which are either obvious things to see or can easily become so. But actually, most names are exactly so because they come from the days when people were named after their professions, or places they lived near, or after well-known things. My own full name, for instance, means "Beautiful, handsome, little river crossing". Not all names tell us what people are really like, I guess... Nevertheless, the 'Powell' of my name would have originated from someone who lived near a river crossing or was associated with it in some way. You'll find then that many names hand you things to see on a plate, which makes the job of memorising considerably easier.

EXERCISE:

There's almost certainly someone in your life you can't remember the name of. A classmate? A teacher or lecturer at the place where you study? A distant relative? Your new neighbours who moved in last month and now you're too embarrassed to ask their name again?

Whatever, when you come across a new person, have a go at memorising their name. If you're really stuck, next time you go to a shop or bank and see an employee with a name tag, have a go at trying to memorise them. Remember – don't stare! Often name tags just give their first name. That's ok – one less thing to have to remember. First names are almost always the most important anyway.

Chapter 8 – Taking it further

Well, you've learned the principle of turning information to be remembered into memory stories. You've learned how to turn numbers and strange alphabets into visual objects you can see. You've even learned how to memorise faces and names. This covers you for almost everything you have to learn at school, college, University…and in life. The only kinds of things I've not covered are poetry recital from memory (which no one requires of you these days unless you're an actor) and memorising sheet music (which may well be a separate book one day, but certainly isn't required of anyone in most education systems around the world until college level). Otherwise, it's all done. System learned. What next? *Plenty.*

But some of you will be wavering. Some will have already dismissed this system thinking it doesn't work (thirty years of using it and teaching hundreds of others to use it successfully proves you wrong), and others will be sceptical. You have gone through a quite a disparate set of memory stories in these pages and may be bewildered by them. Perhaps, already, you can't quite remember what happens after the angry, red-faced man, or what happens after the butler reaches the tin roof shed, or it's Anita *who*? And perhaps language learning held no interest at all and just looked like I put strange squiggles on things which were already strange squiggles?

Well to all of you I say – **NO ONE LIKES YOU ANYWAY, LOSERS**!

No, no…only joking. Honest.

What I do say is this: put it into practice and see what happens anyway. Revising using memory stories requires something of a paradigm shift – a total change in how you think 'study' and 'learning' and 'exams' are supposed to work. In the exercises I've given with each chapter, you might have found it difficult to think of memory stories at all. But don't worry – read ***'Tussling it out'*** below about that.

On the other hand, many of you *will* be using this system and seeing its benefits – which is great! I'd love to hear about your successes, so please do follow me on social media and let me know where things have gone well. But there's a danger there. Sometimes, successful use of memory stories can lead to a problem. I deal with this in the first section: ***'Memorising the Memory Stories'***. I put this first because it is *so important.* Make sure you read it properly.

You may find that, once you've memorised a set of facts, later on there's more information you need to add in. Worry not – that is dealt with in ***'Adding details'***.

Lastly, I promised, way back at the beginning, that you could even use your friends to help you learn stuff *and* help them too in the process. I deal with this at the end. Finally, being with your mates is *good* for studying!

Memorising the Memory Stories – the final stage of exam preparation!

If you've worked through making memory stories and revised regularly (using the *1:1:1 method*?) and been at it a few months now, you should be finding that large chunks of information are just *known*. Even if you're studying history and have long lists of dates of events you've been memorising, there will quickly be a large proportion of them that you simply know. Well done – the synaptic links are now firmly embedded in your brain.

But beware the mistake of thinking they are now part of your permanent memory and you can stop using the memory stories. Don't get me wrong – the whole system is designed to give you maximum speed, ease and efficiency at getting this stuff into your permanent memory, and once it is then of course you don't need the memory stories anymore. Once the house is built, you take down the scaffolding, right?

Not before that exam you don't.

The problem is, as I pointed out at the beginning, that memory just doesn't shuffle from the 'Short Term' box into the 'Long Term' box as traditional psychology teaches. It's a continuous line and even the most fixed memories like your home language and how to walk can start to disintegrate if they aren't used for long periods. There's a real danger that, in the emotional adrenaline rush of the exam, that which you thought was securely memorised will just go *'POOF!'* in the moment and you won't have a memory story rehearsed to claw it back.

Instead what you do is this:

Actively practise the memory stories.

By this I mean, when you're revising the lists of things you've memorised, you can leap straight into the actual information first *and then* rehearse the memory story linked to it afterwards. Effectively, you're reversing the original process of memory story, then interpreting what it means.

Going back to our Reactivity Series, you might now be thinking *"I know that Platinum comes first, followed by Gold, then silver, then copper. My story for this is the butler holding the plate for platinum, with a gold cup pouring into the silver one, and then removing the copper coin from inside the silver cup."* And so on.

This is actually an excellent way to assess how ready you are for the exam. As memories start to become fluent and instant, you can transfer over the order of rehearsal. When testing yourself (Does tin come first or iron?), if the answer isn't instant, you kick into your memory story and find the answer there. When the answer *is* instant (and accurate, of course) then you know you're ready.

Your ideal state to reach for any particular exam is that there is nothing left where you need the memory story any longer and now you are actively revising the stories for the sake of the stories and not because you need them to provide you the recall you need. Then you are absolutely covered for the exam itself. You will have the confidence to get on and shine in that exam but, if suddenly something eludes you, you'll have those memory stories all shiny and engines purring like a tiger, ready to leap into action at a moment's notice should you need to check some detail. There's a good chance that, as you start to use the memory story, the information you need will suddenly pop *back* into your head before you reach it in the story. Such is the weirdness of our neural networks! The point is, having the stories ready gives you the confidence to go into the exam without being nervous that your mind will go blank and nothing will stick.

Tussling it out

A common problem, especially at the beginning of using these techniques, is that of trying to think of things which you can see well enough and will actually remind you of the information you need to recall. It can feel like you're spending ages trying to think of words which help you remember the major veins and arteries of the human body, and you can worry that really you'd be better off just doing the traditional thing of copying them out hundreds of times instead.

Don't make this mistake. The concentration you're putting in to 'tussling it out' is well worth the effort and, more importantly, is helping you make the synaptic link stronger. While you're concentrating on what the best objects, or actions, are to go with whatever terms or words you're learning, you are focusing on that piece of information and doing so much better than a glancing over, or writing out, from traditional methods of just 'reading the book'. Make the effort, it isn't wasted – far from it.

Adding details

Sometimes, you will memorise some information and then find you actually need to add more details. If you adopt this system as your system for life, as I have, then you might find that what you memorised for, say, Biology, at 16 now needs to be deepened when studying at 18, and you might need to go even further when training at university at a level deeper still. Does that mean you have to start from scratch with a new memory story? No, not at all – unless you want to, of course.

When you spend time in a new town or city and get used to going to some particular places, you don't get all confused about those places when you go somewhere new in that town or city, do you? You don't find, after going to the shop for several days, that now you have no idea how to get there because you went to the cinema for the first time. Instead, going to the cinema is just added to your steadily growing map of where places are, that is forming in your mind.

Likewise, you can add details to your memory stories without any problem. I've talked a little about this with the *Tube Map* technique, but we should have a go at doing this for real here. If you've not already got *'The Butler'* story memorised, go back to page 69 now and get the story mastered. It doesn't take too long to get it fixed.

The story is about the reactivity series of metals – when they react, they 'kick' each other out in reactions according to where they are in the series. Potassium is just about as reactive as it gets and rules supreme. Platinum is as dead as a dead thing. But another part of most Chemistry syllabuses is to know so-called 'flame tests'. When you set fire to various chemicals, the colour of the flame will tell you which metals are present. These colour tests are a nightmare for many students because it is so hard to remember them all. Furthermore, as you go up the series, there comes a point where metals will react purely with acid and then later, purely with water (again, potassium, lobbed into a beaker of water is impressive – if you've never seen it, go look it up on Youtube). I'm going to add the flame tests – putting them in in the right place in the series – and the points where acid and water take over to the original story. The new details I will highlight **in bold**.

Picture, if you would, a nicely dressed butler looking very Jeeves and Wooster, carrying dull grey platinum serving plate in one hand. On the plate are some gold goblets and in those are some silver coins, although our Jeeves notices one stray copper coin which he flicks out as a reject. ***When the coin hits the ground it turns a beautiful blue-green colour (copper – blue-green)*** *He starts to move and you notice he is gliding – in fact his feet don't even touch the ground! He's lighter than air…*

It's just as well he's floating because the blue-green ground seems to be bubbling and hissing away – it's become acid! (Everything from now on reacts with acids). *You realise he's going to float away if you're not careful so you tie lead weights to his ankles which help bring him back down. He walks/floats over to a tin-roofed shed and goes inside. Within he sees a man ironing a shirt (perhaps the butler's?) but the man realises he made a mark on the shirt and takes it over to a grey-coloured sink to try and wash it. He scrubs the shirt with what he thinks is a scrubbing brush but it's actually a piece of coal! Now, he's made a real mess and is angry with the coal.*

He wraps up the coal in kitchen foil and gets out a light to set fire to it. When he does this, it turns out he's lit a fuse which burns distinctly until it reaches the wrapped-up silver ball and it then explodes. ***Because of the explosion, the fire alarm sprinkler turns on for a moment giving a brief shower of rain (everything from now on reacts with water).*** *A chalky white powdery substance falls down like snow and the man rushes to grab a glass to collect some of it.* ***While the snow falls, he tries setting fire to it with a lighter and there's two little puffs of explosion and instantly an orange and a red brick are conjured out of mid-air (Calcium – orange-brick red) As he moves to collect more of the chalky snow in a glass, he knocks a metal BAR on the floor and two apples roll out of it***

(Barium – apple green). He wonders if this really is chalk and thinks it might be salt to use in his dinner, so he picks up a yellow stone (lithium is yellow and means stone, lithos from Greek) and a small boy tries to repeat his trick of setting fire to it with a lighter. He's furious at the boy and screams at him to go away with his face a bright red (Lithium – red). *He tastes the chalk he collected – it is indeed salt! Perfect for his dinner. He goes to the stove where there is a pot of something bubbling away and pours the salt into it.* ***The food instantly turns yellow (Sodium – yellow). He checks the flames under the pot are still keeping it warm enough underneath. How weird! Little purple lilac flowers are springing up where the flames should be! (Potassium – lilac). Oh well!*** *Perhaps the butler, who has observed all this, will serve up this strange meal on his dish later?*

There – it wasn't too hard to make minor adjustments to the story and insert extra scenes. Revise the story two or three times and you will find the new parts quickly become as well known as the rest. We actually added *eight* new facts in there.

Working in pairs or groups

The traditional way of thinking is that you should study alone. To be fair, I remember doing my A levels back in the 80s and having several weeks of 'revision parties' where around eight or nine of us who were close friends crashed out at a mate's house while his parents were away and, allegedly, we studied. In reality, *some* study got done, but mostly it was spent mucking around. Most of us are still friends now and there is, somewhere, a damning photo of what looks like me throwing an actual brick at someone. You can see it, perfectly captured in mid-air and the evidence is clear it is me chucking it. I say now, for the record, that the brick was a joke one made of sponge. But I will need to pay my friends large bribes if I ever become famous and I want to keep that picture out of the newspapers!

But I digress. The point is, if you're going to 'study' with your friends and you know full well you'll just end up larking around – don't do it! But, the *TNTL Memory Story* method can actually help you to work well with your friends, help them too *and* have fun.

Firstly, persuade them to buy this book (heh, heh) and then make sure they know and understand the system well. Choose friends who are doing the same subjects as you and, if you need to, have different study parties with different friends to study different subjects. My mistake, back in my youth, was that we were all studying completely different subjects and even different levels of exams.

Research has shown that students learn more and remember more if they have been testing each other. It is a great way to do things. In a traditional form, one of you would have the textbook and just fire off questions from the text – and this is good! It will work. But even better (and more fun) is to spend time coming up with memory stories together – the sillier, the better – and have a good giggle coming up with them. Laughter is great. It's emotion, it's pleasant, and it helps form good synaptic links. Then, test each other on the very things you are all trying to memorise and see how you do. Trust me, this is the most fun you can have with studying that's actually productive and useful. You can do this in pairs or in groups of three, four, five...actually I don't know if there's an upper limit. After all, I was often doing this with my students, with as many as ten or more in the class and we had an absolute gas. I'm fairly certain some students actually, literally, fell off their chairs sometimes...

Try not to laugh

My last section raised an excellent point to finish with for this little book. The *TNTL Memory Story* system will always work best if it is fun. Unless you decide to work in groups, your stories are private and just for you. Sometimes the words you come up with might be rude – I won't judge you. The things that happen might be rude – I don't care.

You might have people you know, love and/or respect doing outrageous things – I give you permission. The sillier it is, the more you will remember it – and that's the bottom line.

But…

When it comes to that exam; when you're sat in invigilation silence, not allowed to do anything to disturb or raise suspicion of cheating; when you're searching back in your mind and going through a needed memory story. Please. Please…

Try not to laugh.

EXERCISE:

It's time for you to go it alone. You know everything you need so that you can memorise anything you so desire with the minimum of time and effort and maximum of confidence it won't be forgotten when you need it. If you want a little more practise at all this (particularly the number system aspect) then go look at the appendix for some cool applications which can be used for fun and entertainment with family, friends and perhaps even to impress some teachers.

But most of all, get using it on all the things you need or want to memorise. Give it a go, and message me on social media if you need extra help or advice. As much as I can, I will try to help! Get in contact too, if there are things missing in this book you'd like to see included in future editions. I consider all suggestions seriously and will endeavour to make improvements where I can.

Good luck!

Final checklist:

- Have you properly understood the information you want to memorise?
- Have you made sure your diet is balanced, exercise is regular and manageable, and water intake is correct?
- Are you getting enough sleep?
- Have you made sure your working environment is as good as it can be? Have you factored in walking and refreshment breaks?
- Have you taken the time to learn the *Memory Story* system? Including memory palace, tube map, consonant and peg systems?
- Have you made sure you're following the 1:1:1 method or similar to make sure all memory stories are regularly practised?
- Have you made sure your images are as silly and memorable as possible? Have you used the double entry method where possible to give your memories extra back up?

Appendix – Tricks

Pi to 20 decimal places (and beyond...)

Do you often wonder what follows after the first 3.14 in the value of the Pi? Let me introduce you to a great little memory trick which is easy to memorise and quick to perform so you won't bore people. Twenty decimal places is usually more than enough to impress though if you memorise further you can claim you can do more (and your spectators will often ask you to prove it!). More importantly, it will give you good practice at having recurring numbers in your memory story. There's none in the first twenty places but two crop up in the ten after that.

The Story

Sitting in a tree you notice a large tower spring up beside you. You decide to take a look and go inside where you see a doll being played with by none other than Mr Bean himself! He has been thrown in jail which is very bare but he does at least receive the mail from the postman. You see this happen and note he gets a calendar which he puts up on the month of February. Looking at it happily, Mr Bean starts drinking from a cup until a strange man takes it off him. The man is dressed like one of the mafia who has come to scare Mr Bean, blindfolding him with a dirty rag... (The man then nudges him further into the cell where there is a ram bleating away. More men from the mafia now appear and they all have the face of the original man. They now all hold out new cups to Mr Bean – they're here for a party! One of them reaches into his pocket and realises he is losing his knife, because the jacket is on fire. He takes it off and puts it on top of a large cot that's there in the cell.)

Here's the actual numbers for reference:

3.14 15 92 65 35 89 79 32 38 46 (26 43 38 32 79 50 28 84 19 71)

The Knight's Tour

The *Knight's Tour* is a classic puzzle much beloved by computer programmers who love working out algorithms to solve it. There are many solutions but try doing it for yourself without using one and you'll see it is fiendishly difficult to do.

The basic premise is that the knight from a chess piece has the most complex move of all the pieces. It moves two squares in one direction and then turns either left or right from there and moves one more square. The result is the telltale L-shape. The *Knight's Tour challenge* is to place the knight on an empty chessboard and move it using this legal move until you have covered all 64 squares. The difficulty is doing it without landing on any square more than once.

1	2	3	4	5	6	7	8
9	10	11	12	13	14	15	16
17	18	19	20	21	22	23	24
25	26	27	28	29	30	31	32
33	34	35	36	37	38	39	40
41	42	43	44	45	46	47	48
49	50	51	52	53	54	55	56
57	58	59	60	61	62	63	64

That's usually as far as most solutions take it, but our memory story method allows us to do what only magicians are able to do (I recall first seeing this trick performed on the *Paul Daniels Magic Show* when I was a kid). We can have our backs turned (or be blindfolded for extra drama) and a volunteer, who will move the piece for you and cross off the squares as you go, will place the knight on any square they wish. As long as you're told which square it is, you'll be good to go and perform this little miracle.

This isn't just a super magic trick to perform, the memory story is one of the longest you're likely to ever come across which can really hone your skills. Likewise, it covers the numbers 1-64 – which is a good chunk to remember! – and will give you valuable practice to make these fluent. Just for fun I've given one example of 'double entry' – can you spot it? After the story, I've given a complete list of all the numbers in order. Read down the columns for each block of 32 separately.

The Story

You are walking towards a gate and notice there is a nameplate on it made of metal, perhaps with your name engraved on it. You take some drum sticks out of your pocket and begin tapping a rhythm out on the metal. The noise attracts a small dog which comes over and obediently sits on a mat when you tell it to. The dog then starts chewing on a nut but that annoys you and you walk away through a door. It's worse on the other side though as there's a hen clucking away!

You pick up the hen and see that it has nails sticking out of it, which you remove and decide it needs a bath in a tub to clean up the wounds. When you've finished cleaning the hen you take it out of the tub and put little shoes on it to protect its feet. You put it onto the ground which is actually wooden decking so you can hear its shoes clomping away. Then you can't resist it any longer, you want to eat it so you pick up the hen and try to wring its neck but all it does is squawk loudly. You fear you'll be caught stealing someone's chicken so you begin to run away in the rain hiding in a cupboard and locking the door. Unfortunately, where you've hidden yourself has a lid above and something takes the lid off to expose you…

Thankfully, it's just an old mare and, using a mop in with you, you climb out through the top and find you've come up in a secret science lab. There you see someone experimenting on raw meat and when you look closely you see it is God himself doing the experimenting, all the time wiping his brow, sweating with concentration, with a rag. He picks up his mug for a drink but it is empty, so he shouts to his assistant – a lamb – to make a fresh pot!

The lamb assistant glues the mug to the wall using gum it was chewing before then leaving the room to go to a rave party next door. You follow and see lots of men dressed as the mafia. One of them comes up to you and hands you a white lily and in return you try to give him a red rose back. But he starts to run off before you can do so and you chase him with a rose in hand into a huge maze. You find your way to the centre where there is a huge waterfall dammed up by twigs and rubbish. You use a knife to cut it all free…

…and find there is a ram that has been stuck inside all this time! It runs off bleating, straight to the side of your mum who is scowling at you, blaming you unfairly for the state of the ram. She starts to pick out lice which have infested its coat and places them into envelopes ready to mail off later. But then a rat starts to nibble at the envelopes! You laugh loudly at this which gets your mum very angry. She makes you line up with other naughty children and a man passes a mic to each of you in turn to confess your misdeeds publicly…

…But you run away and escape by dressing as a nun and end up floating up to heaven by being so holy! But when you get there you find everyone is, strangely, gnawing at their clothes and anything else they can find, so you decide to float back down to earth only to find a mob angry with your previous escape coming to bring you to justice, armed with logs in their hands. At gunpoint you are loaded into a train which runs on rails to take you back – but at least on the way you get to listen to nice, relaxing jazz!

You are brought before a judge who represents the Law and he is so old and inhuman he can take out his jaw to use it as a gavel to bang on his desk. He is angry when he sees you and throws a rock at you which hits a man holding a doll innocently sat in the seats watching proceedings. The doll was damaged by the rock and cracks open.

Bees start flying out – it's a beehive! Everyone panics as angry bees swarm around. One flies up your nose and, in your panic to get it out, you start scraping your nose against a tree...

Finally, things calm down and you sit by this tree to enjoy the setting sun with a nice glass of wine in your hand. You're drifting off nicely when someone nudges you – it's your dad! He's come to offer you some food – a nice bread bun. Before you can take it, a dove flies down and grabs the bun taking it off to a nearby den. You trot off to retrieve it and find lots of things in the den. You pick up a door knob and realise you know where this goes – it is the missing knob to get into your tower! You head there and attach it to the door to open and find inside leads to a big field where you find a gate with a name plate on it...and so the story begins again.

8	gate	25	nail	34	mare	63	gum
23	name	19	tub	49	mop	48	rave
6	sticks	2	shoe	59	lab	38	mafia
16	dog	17	deck	44	raw	55	lily
31	mat	27	neck	61	God	40	rose
21	nut	42	run/rain	46	rag	30	maze
4	door	57	lock	36	mug	13	dam
10	hen	51	lid	53	lamb	28	knife

43	ram	22	nun	54	law	9	wine
33	mum	7	heaven	64	jaw	26	nudge
50	lice	24	gnaw	47	rock	11	dad
35	mail	39	mob	32	man	1	bun
41	rat	56	log	15	doll	18	dove
58	laugh	62	gun	5	hive	12	den
52	line	45	rail	20	nose	29	knob
37	mic	60	jazz	3	tree	14	tower

Memorising a deck of cards

In this trick, someone can hand you a shuffled deck of cards and, after flipping through the cards just once, spending no more than a second or two on each, you can recite the order, have the deck cut to any card and say what comes before and after, locate a card from any position and a host of other ways of showing off your memory. You don't even need to memorise a full deck if you wish – have a clump chosen, shuffled and then quickly run through them once and reveal the names any way you wish.

This trick is, in some ways, the hardest of tricks because you have 52 distinct items to remember and they are going to come to you in a completely random order each time. You'll also be under a time pressure which means getting a memory story fixed at speed, without mistakes, first time.

On the plus side, this uses variations of the consonant system which should be familiar to you by now and, with a few practices, these memory items should become pretty fluent, making the trick much easier and giving you another way to entrench the consonant system to make it easy to use.

Below is the list of items to attach as an image for each card, As always, you're free to substitute your own items if you can think of something better or more memorably personal to you. Down the left side you'll see the cards of each suit, from Ace down to King. Along the top, you'll see the suits – Clubs, Heart, Spades and Diamonds. The images are formed mostly by using the consonant system to create a letter for the number followed by C, S or D. The court cards just use their own J, Q or K sounds.

You'll notice I missed out H for Hearts. That's because it is quite difficult to find words which end in H which don't need an S or C and changes the sound – which could result in confusing the suits. Instead, I've thought of H as an almost silent letter and therefore gone for words which end in a kind of 'open vowel' sound. You'll get used to it but, basically, when you have an item which doesn't end in a consonant – it's a Heart!

Another issue is that the consonant system doesn't include 10 but we have one in the values. I've borrowed from the simple system here and thought of 10 as 'hen' but shortened that to a simple H. All tens, therefore, start in H. Again, feel free to change this if you don't like it.

One final point to add is that we have TWO clashes with the court cards. J is also a 6 under the consonant system and K is a 7. To get around this, all items for Jacks and Kings begin with literal J's and K's but 6's begin with G and 7's begin with a hard C (still giving the 'k' sound but spelt with a C). You'll need to be wary of this to begin with but, after a few practices, these items will become fairly fluent and you'll no longer need to worry about it.

	C	H	S	D
Ace = t/d	Duck	Toe	Taste	Ted(dy)
2 = n	Neck	Noah	Nose	Nod
3 = m	Mac	Ma	Moss	Mud
4 = r	Rock	Row	Rice	Rod
5 = l	Lock	Law	Lice	Lad

6 = g	Gecko	Go	Geese	God
7 = c	Cook	Car	Cuss	Cod
8 = f	Fox	Foe	Fish	Fed
9 = b	Book	Bow	Bass (guitar)	Bed
10 = h	Hook	Hoe	Horse	Head
J	Joke	Jar	Joss stick	Jade
Q	Quick	Queer	Quest	Quid
K	Kick	Key	Kiss	Kid

As an example of how a story might look, I'll share one I did in preparation for writing this. I grabbed a handful of cards (33 in total), shuffled them, and whizzed through them just once. The story will be spectacularly bizarre but, hopefully, you'll see it is easily memorised.

I'm holding a ROD (4D) and using it to spread out a MAC (3C) on the ground. I accidentally hit a ROCK (4C) which bounces up and lodges in my NOSE (2S). I dislodge it but a nosebleed ensues, weirdly not of blood but RICE (4S) pouring from my nostril. But I use a KEY (KH) to tighten up my head and stop the 'bleeding'. Done with that, I KICK (KC) the key to a woman who is marching on a QUEST (QS). She hands the key to a trusted KID (KD) who puts the key into a slot in his NECK (2C) for safekeeping. After a while he passes it on to his MA (3H) who is COOKing (7C). But in the pan is a JADE (JD) jewel which she feels should be given to the judge who represents the LAW (5H) and he orders her to GO (6H). The reason? It is dangerous – he's going to fight his FOE (8H). He does this using a JAR (JH) as a weapon and then notices this jar was LOCKed (5C) to the Biblical character of NOAH (2H) who finds the whole thing funny – in fact, it's a real JOKE (JC) to him. He's rather foul, picking and flicking LICE (5S) from his beard while trying to KISS (KS) a young girl standing nearby. How strange! She NODs (2D) her consent for him to do so – yuck! But only if she can light a JOSS stick (JS) she has to mask his horrid smell. Before either can happen, a young man – a LAD (5D), in fact – comes up and woos her away. He takes her FISHing (8S) and they sit on a nice patch of MOSS (3S) by a river to watch the DUCKs (AC) go by. The boy changes his mind about fishing and decides to ROW (4H) his sweetheart in a boat up the river – aww, how romantic! But when she gets in, she sees the boat is full of GECKOs (6C) which splash out of the boat and into the MUD (3D) in panic. Some of the mud splashes onto her pretty dress and she CUSSes (7S) the lad for causing this to happen. He tries to placate her but only succeeds when he offers her a British QUID (QD).

Acknowledgements

I have already thanked the students of LAMB English Medium School, Bangladesh in my dedication, but I will say it again here. You were all so much fun and coped with this *oddbhut bideshi* and his strange ways, yet never failed to be loving, kind and ready to work hard for me. I remember our days of laughter with such fondness it brings tears to my eyes. I miss you all.

During those years at LAMB I was able to dedicate whole lessons to the art of memorising and this was so useful, both for the students and for the development of this book, that I must thank the Headmaster, Mr Christian Vestergaard, for accepting my request and fitting these sessions into the timetable which was already stretched to limit. I am tremendously grateful.

I will also be eternally grateful to the teacher who eventually replaced me at LAMB. Known so universally as "Auntie Charlotte" that I can find no one who actually remembers her surname, the afore-mentioned Auntie Charlotte was a wonderful inspiration to me, coming into teaching under very difficult conditions in her retirement. For years after I left, she badgered me about writing this book and even offered to help fund it if needed. It will be to my everlasting shame that I was not able to complete it in time to help her as she took many students through their exams. Had she not constantly cajoled me though, this book may never have been written at all.

I am grateful to my assistant who checked, edited and helped organise the mess of material I had written to get it into some kind of order. Aditi Chandak, I could not have done this without you and I'm very grateful to you for all your help and encouragement. Aditi is also a published author in her own right, so do look her up!

I'm grateful too for my daughter Jess who uses these methods herself in her own academic work and reminds me of what I already know but can sometimes doubt – that these techniques really work whether you're twelve or twenty. At the time of writing, she's at university and still using these techniques.

Finally, this book wouldn't be half as much fun or useful as it is had I not had access to a super artist to do my cover and illustrations. Sangeetha Alwar is a super-talented human being and, when she's not being brilliant at illustrations, is also a fully qualified professor of English and, therefore, should probably have been the one to write this book. For the fact that she didn't, I can only apologise.

About the Author – D K Powell

D K Powell is a freelance writer, educationalist and social activist living in the UK but working around the world. He is the author of the acclaimed ***Sonali*** (2016), the bestselling ***The Old Man on the Beach***, has written several educational courses on psychology, sociology, and related subjects, and has contributed chapters to numerous educational and academic books. His articles are regularly published in major publications all over the world. His novel, ***The Pukur***, will be published by Histria Books in 2022.

He has lived and worked all over the world as an educational consultant, both training teachers and teaching students, predominantly in Asia. While living in Bangladesh he developed an insatiable appetite for *cha* which continues to the present day.

D K Powell writes and speaks on social and cultural issues internationally but also writes as a journalist and reviewer for national newspapers, magazines and web media outlets. His TEDx talk on ***'Why we need to embrace the Global Village'*** has been watched over 40,000 times and he is in demand as a guest speaker. He continues to give training and advice to education providers throughout Asia and is available for speaking engagements or consultancy advice.

Email: ***dkpowell.contact@gmail.com***.

Twitter: @DKenPowell

Facebook: D K Powell

Instagram: kendkpowell

About the Illustrator – Sangeetha Alwar

An English professor by day and a Quasi-Modo look-alike while hunched over her iPad, Sangeetha spends most of her free time making art. A self-taught artist, she illustrates the world around her. She takes her humour like she takes her coffee - dark.

Find Sangeetha on **Instagram:** ***@ms.alwar***.

Notes

Title:

Lists

-
-
-

Doodles

Title:

Lists

-
-
-

Doodles

Title: ______________________________

Lists

•
•
•

Doodles

Title: ______

Lists

-
-
-

Doodles

Printed in Great Britain
by Amazon

14053229R00084